All drawings done with BIC
metalpoint roller pens.
Book Design: Jim Romano
Type: Optext
Stats: Tony Mistretta
Printing: Arizona Lithographers
Paper: Lewis Paper Co.

Other books by Bill Olendorf:

Addison Mizner, Architect to the Affluent (1983)
Palm Beach Sketchbook (1988)

Library of Congress Cataloging in Publication Data

1. Chicago 2. Architecture, Chicago School 3. Art, Chicago
I. Olendorf, Bill II. Tolf, Robert W. III. Title
1988 88-92663
ISBN 0-923078-00-2

Printed in the United States of America

0 9 8 7 6 5 4 3 2 1

9 E. Ontario Chicago, IL 60611
(312) 787-6501

CHICAGO
SKETCHBOOK

by BILL OLENDORF
text by ROBERT TOLF

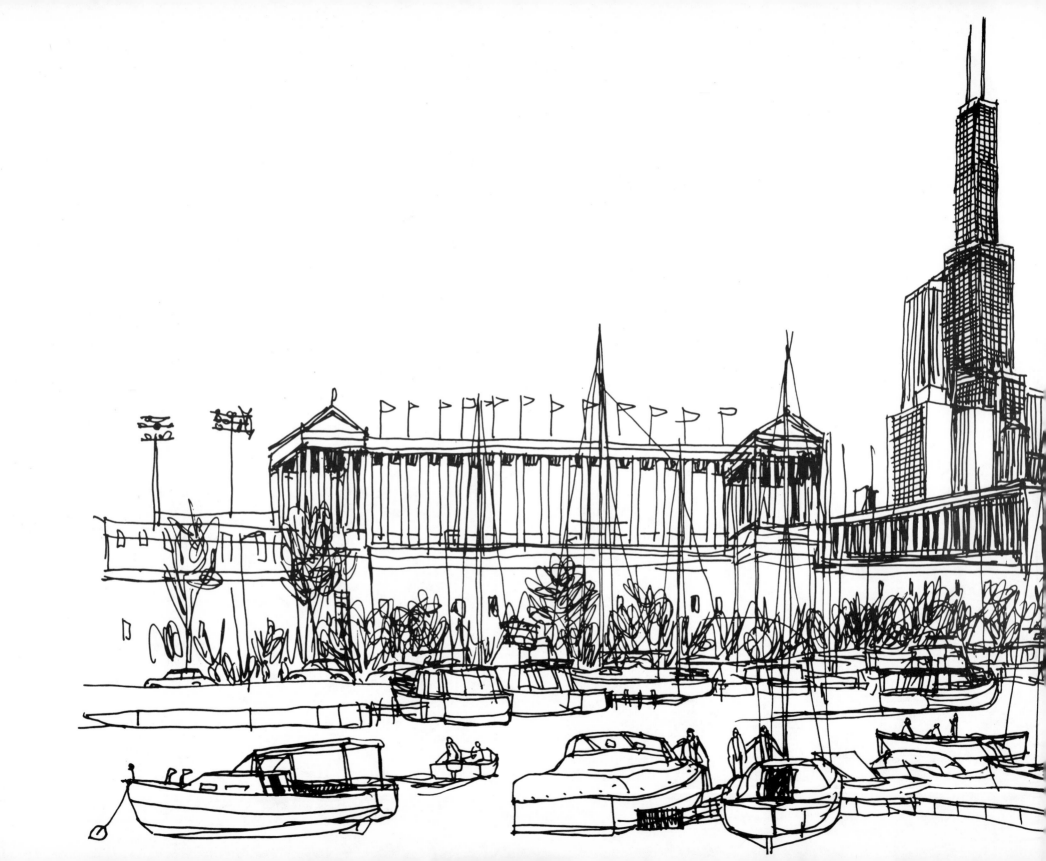

Table of Contents

INTRODUCTION

Another book on Chicago?

You bet!

Different from the rest and maybe the best. A personal statement showing the sweep and sheer power of a city of firsts, mosts, greatests. A city of catalysts with incredible entrepreneurial energies—"Chicago's a great place to make money," a Pakistani cabdriver told us recently—and the fastest growing city in the history of the world.

Birthplace of McDonald's and *Playboy,* of the mail order business and the skyscraper. Chewing gum capital of the world and home of Baby Ruth and Brach's, Reed's Butterscotch, Snickers and Mars bars—and Cracker Jack.

Then there's "Sweetness" himself—the Bears' Walter Payton—and a long, long list of legendary sports heroes.

Railhead, collector and processor of cattle, lumber and grain; trading center with steel mills and stock yards. An elemental, open-heart metropolis dominating the Midwest, but an elegant one as well, with the world's finest symphony orchestra and its finest art museum and university.

Of course we need another book on Chicago!

PRELUDE

From my first moments of life at the Swedish Covenant Hospital over on Foster Avenue to my last Wait Till Next Year cry for the Cubs, I'm a Chicagoan through and through, tried and true.

The origins go back to the banner year of 1860. Lincoln was nominated in Chicago and my grandmother was born in Chicago. And she spun the stories of the early days to a fascinated boy who was gaining a hands-on, do-it-yourself education in the museum minestrone of magic and marvels, and along the streets and sidewalks of the city's ethnic exotica.

The great architectural achievements were experienced—as a matter of everyday existence, with a father in The Rookery, a grandfather in the Board of Trade, a father-in-law in the Continental Bank Building (his first job in 1910 was in the Manhattan Building), and other family members earning their daily bread in other monuments of the Loop. A summer was spent wrecking and rebuilding the Marshall Field Warehouse for Pepper Construction Company—with cousin Dick Pepper; his father owned the company.

I had an Orphan Annie decoder ring, got up at dawn to be at Don McNeil's Breakfast Club, and cheered on Kukla, Fran and Ollie, those quintessential Chicago expressions. And I braved the Century of Progress sky-ride, the Bobs at Riverview and applauded the best of Broadway at the Shubert and Civic Opera, and devoted entire afternoons working my way up to the front rows for the stage shows at the Oriental and Chicago theaters. Then there was the beauty of the open air concerts at Grant Park and Ravinia, the swimming, fishing and boating on Lake Michigan; the pilgrimages to the homes of my heroes—Phil Cavaretta and Andy Pafko, Luke Appling and Nellie Fox, Ernie Banks, Butkus, Bronco, Bulldog Turner and Sid Luckman.

Just about the time I learned how to spell the name of Bear fullback Gary Famiglietti, I discovered the joys of Chicago's own version of pizza, a deep-dish delight. And emptied the cornucopia of culinary excitement that has for years made the city one of the eating capitals of the world.

Of course I went to the Empire Room after the Senior Prom.

And where else would I spend my wedding night than the Drake?

Chicago! You ARE a wonderful town!

Robert Tolf

Robert Tolf

WORDS FROM THE ARTIST:

Chicago—to know it is to love it! I've been almost everywhere on earth, why do I always look forward to coming home to Chicago?

Because it's something special! It has an excitement, a beauty all its own. It is a cultural oasis where people are civilized (well, most of them) and truly the best place in America to live (except in the winter).

Chicagoans smile, laugh at themselves, and go out of their way to help visitors (where else in America?). We call it culture shock.

We have our problems, but I agree with the guy who said, "The toilets flush, the streets are clean, and the Cubs haven't left town." Chicago does not seem to change, in a changing world.

This book was on the drawing board for lots of years. It was a labor of love for both Bob Tolf and myself. We both came from here, and so did our families for two generations. We both enjoyed the documentation of our relatives in Chicago's past, even if it was just part of the big picture at that time.

THANK YOU, THANK YOU, THANK YOU!

Thanks to so many folks who cheered this effort on…

This includes Karl Kroc for his early enthusiasm, Andrew McNally's advice and approval, Art Schultz for those appreciated but non-productive calls to the Art Institute. Des Paden's efforts to sell the package, Paul Young's help in early financial performance projections, Irwin Noparstak's accounting advice, plus Chris Photakis' and Laurie Veda's faith and help in details, for background information and being kind at all times. Art Mertz's research and general information was key, as was Bill Hetherington's plans to sell the finished product. Without Tom Moles joining me on many a dawn patrol to locate hidden locations, it just would not have seemed so easy. Thanks also to Doug Ekman, Tony Mistretta and David Dakich for their understanding when I would appear with a request for piles of stats ASAP, to Jim Romano for his talent in putting it all together, and to Elaine Kittredge for her smarts and advice and ability setting type in the best way. Most of all, thanks to Dick Lewis and Lewis Sullivan, my partners, who saw a fun project with an opportunity, and really made it happen. Thanks also to my family, whose patience was appreciated during those endless non-productive and frustrating periods when I went into a spin. And, finally, thanks to you, dear art lover, who have already invested hard-earned cash to be further delighted, amused, enchanted and entertained in this interpretation of what Chicago really is and where it came from. I hope the investment proves to be worthy of the trip. Happy reading!

Pathfinders & Pioneers

In the beginning was a tropical sea, then the glaciers leaving in their frozen wake pool table flat plains with enough water rushing through fissures to make this western tip of a great lake a vital portage point, first for the Indians and then for French traders and trappers, Jolliet, LaSalle, Marquette, and finally a settler, Jean Baptiste Point du Sable, son of a black slave and Canadian merchant.

The French and then the British were in command, but the American Revolution brought the area into the new nation's Northwest Territory and in 1803, the year of the Louisiana Purchase, President Jefferson ordered that a palisaded fort be built on the southern bank of the mouth of the river, astride the watery communications link joining east and west, north and south.

A few hardy pioneers, including John Kinzie—later to be collector of tolls and first president of the village—were attracted to the fort, but when the British again threatened and Indians were aroused in the first year of the War of 1812, the intrepid band was ordered to evacuate and head for Fort Wayne. Fifty-three of the men, women and children never made it. They were attacked and killed by the Indians about a mile and a half from Fort Dearborn—their bodies to remain unburied for another four years, until the war was over.

The soldiers and settlers abandoning Fort Dearborn were ambushed at this point of land, 18th Street and Calumet.

18TH STREET AND CALUMET. SITE OF THE FORT DEARBORN MASSACRE.

Fort Dearborn, an important presence at this site from 1803 until 1857, would be a vastly overshadowed, overwhelmed toy today.

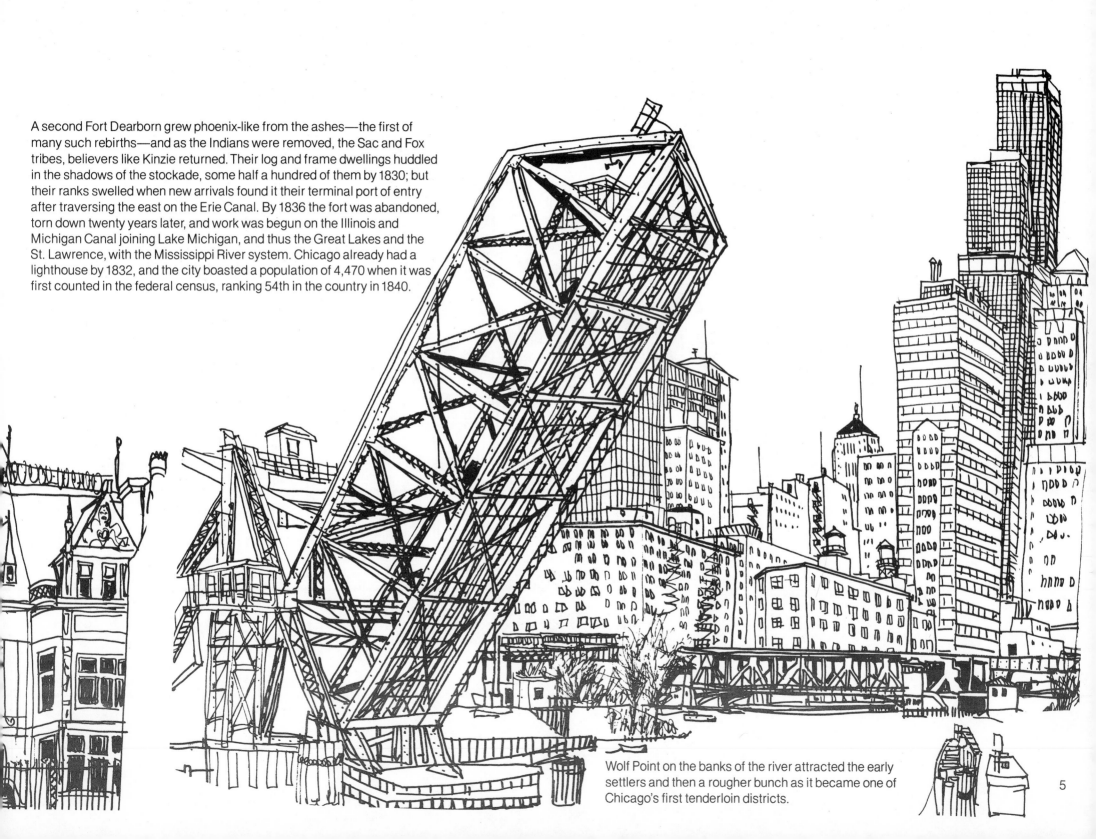

A second Fort Dearborn grew phoenix-like from the ashes—the first of many such rebirths—and as the Indians were removed, the Sac and Fox tribes, believers like Kinzie returned. Their log and frame dwellings huddled in the shadows of the stockade, some half a hundred of them by 1830; but their ranks swelled when new arrivals found it their terminal port of entry after traversing the east on the Erie Canal. By 1836 the fort was abandoned, torn down twenty years later, and work was begun on the Illinois and Michigan Canal joining Lake Michigan, and thus the Great Lakes and the St. Lawrence, with the Mississippi River system. Chicago already had a lighthouse by 1832, and the city boasted a population of 4,470 when it was first counted in the federal census, ranking 54th in the country in 1840.

Wolf Point on the banks of the river attracted the early settlers and then a rougher bunch as it became one of Chicago's first tenderloin districts.

HENRY B. CLARKE HOUSE 1836
1855 S. INDIANA AVENUE.

The year that Fort Dearborn was abandoned, Henry B. Clarke, a prosperous merchant who had arrived from New York with his family in 1833, built an imposing Greek Revival mansion on the south side of the river. It rivaled the residence designed in similar style across the river—home of Chicago's first mayor, William B. Ogden.

Ogden outlived Clarke by 28 years—he perished in one of the city's periodic cholera epidemics—but Clarke's Greek temple survived, forever known as Widow Clarke's House. It was moved by later owners, fearing another Chicago Fire, four miles south to its present location at 4526 South Wabash Avenue.

1857— THE YEAR CHICAGO RAISED THE ROOF

Did Chicago ever raise the roof? Of course. Its broad shoulders also raised entire buildings, such as the Biggs House on the corner of Randolph and Wells Streets in 1857. It was all part of an incredibly ambitious program to improve drainage and eliminate the all-too-often muddy thoroughfares. Its was a twenty-year project with some of the structures being raised as much as a dozen feet, and some of them were as large as the Biggs House—five storeys and thousands of tons. Of course, there were some stubborn souls who refused such heroics, and they remained at the level of quagmire.

BIGGS HOUSE

CLARK STREET 1857

THE RAISING OF BIGGS HOUSE - RANDOLPH & WELLS
1857

JOHN J. GLESSNER
HOUSE, PRAIRIE AVENUE

Chicago, the city of firsts, has an important last—the last building designed by Henry Hobson Richardson, the re-interpreter of Romanesque in 19th Century America. Built for one of the founders of International Harvester, John J. Glessner, it is the finest example in the country of the domestic adaptation of the distinctive style. Today the rough-hewn granite fortress, a shrine for students of the Richardson aesthetic, is owned and operated by the Chicago Architecture Foundation, a spirited and gifted group which organizes pertinent, precedent-setting exhibits and conducts tours of Chicago's architectural arsenal by foot, bus and boat.

Prairie Avenue—now a Historic District—has only a few reminders remaining of its Victorian Gilded Age when the Armours and the Swifts, the Fields, Pullmans and Glessners made it the Gold Coast, a refuge and retreat two miles from the center of town.

PRARIE AVENUE

MAXWELL STREET

And for something completely different, there was Maxwell Street, an open-air, Jewish bazaar with goods of all sizes and sorts for sale by the peddlers and hawkers.

9

JANE ADDAM'S HULL HOUSE
1889

10

A different kind of quagmire was faced by social pioneer Jane Addams, who opened in 1889 Hull House at 800 South Halsted, one of the city's worst neighborhoods.

Inspired by London's Toynbee Hall, the indomitable lady defined the area's dire need as broadly as playgrounds and day care centers—the city's first—and blazed trails in all fields of settlement work, embarrassing city and state officials into action. When she was awarded the Nobel Peace Prize in 1931, two of her most famous Hull House alums, Benny Goodman and the Marx of the Hart, Schaffner and Marx clothing manufacturers, were launching their own careers, and a third, Harold Ickes, was about to start his in Washington.

Two of Jane Addams' original buildings have been restored by the University of Illinois at Chicago and serve now as a vibrant museum tribute to one of Chicago's most famous citizens.

At the other end of the social and economic scale there was Chicago's Society Street, the Prairie Avenue district where such architectural memories as this French Chateau were built for the city's Beautiful People, the newly wealthy merchants, manufacturers, bankers and real estate speculators.

11

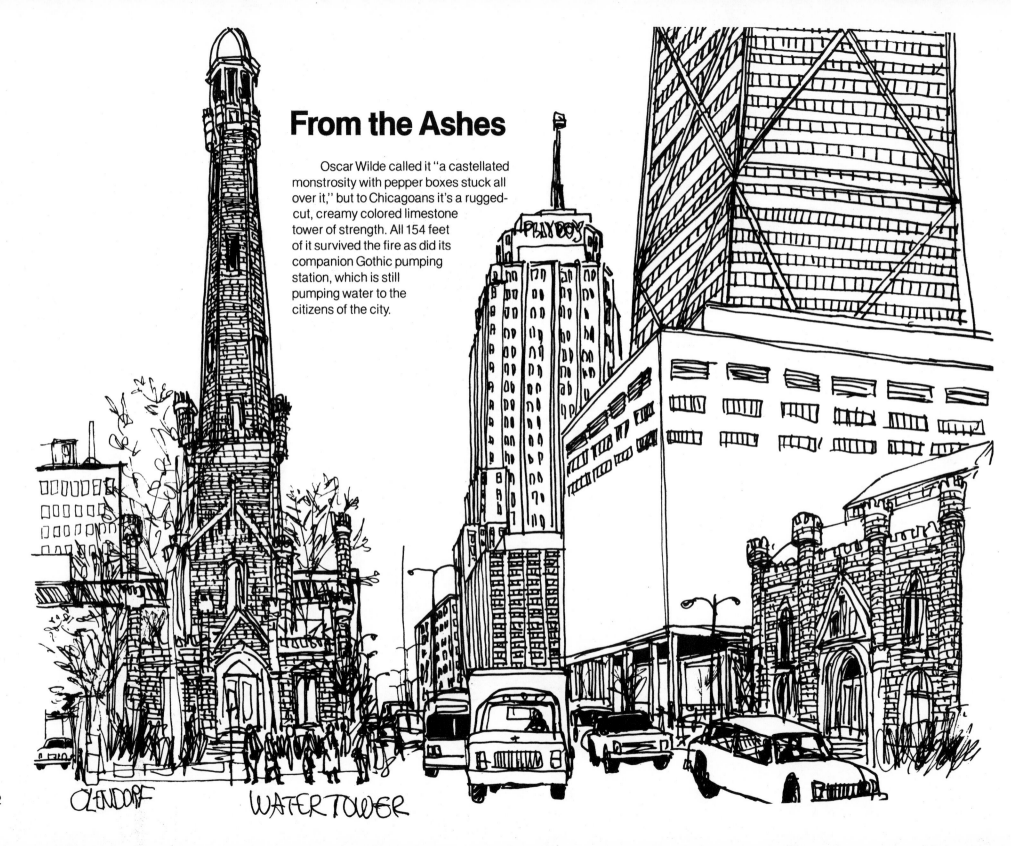

From the Ashes

Oscar Wilde called it "a castellated monstrosity with pepper boxes stuck all over it," but to Chicagoans it's a rugged-cut, creamy colored limestone tower of strength. All 154 feet of it survived the fire as did its companion Gothic pumping station, which is still pumping water to the citizens of the city.

OLENDORF

WATER TOWER

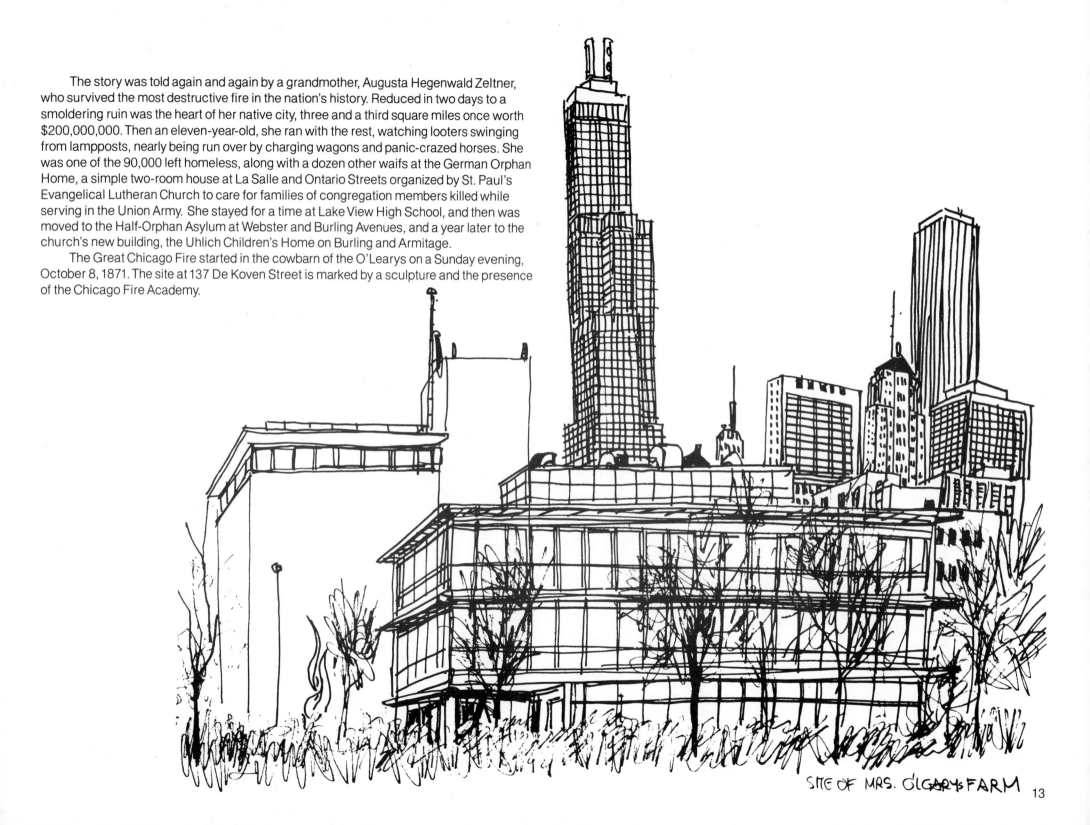

The story was told again and again by a grandmother, Augusta Hegenwald Zeltner, who survived the most destructive fire in the nation's history. Reduced in two days to a smoldering ruin was the heart of her native city, three and a third square miles once worth $200,000,000. Then an eleven-year-old, she ran with the rest, watching looters swinging from lampposts, nearly being run over by charging wagons and panic-crazed horses. She was one of the 90,000 left homeless, along with a dozen other waifs at the German Orphan Home, a simple two-room house at La Salle and Ontario Streets organized by St. Paul's Evangelical Lutheran Church to care for families of congregation members killed while serving in the Union Army. She stayed for a time at Lake View High School, and then was moved to the Half-Orphan Asylum at Webster and Burling Avenues, and a year later to the church's new building, the Uhlich Children's Home on Burling and Armitage.

The Great Chicago Fire started in the cowbarn of the O'Learys on a Sunday evening, October 8, 1871. The site at 137 De Koven Street is marked by a sculpture and the presence of the Chicago Fire Academy.

SITE OF MRS. O'LEARYS FARM

13

Chicago rebuilt—oh how it rebuilt—rousing itself mightily from the ashes, erecting 3000 buildings in 300 working days. And those were brick and stone structures. Thousands of wooden frame buildings were constructed to house the flood of Scandinavians and Germans who came as craftsmen and construction workers, finding a new land of opportunity in the bustling city which worked round the clock—in a never-ceasing excess of lightning-like energy.

Then came the architectural innovators and the engineers who dared to build higher and higher. William Le Baron Jenney, a major on Sherman's staff during the Civil War, designed the world's first iron-and-steel-frame building, the Home Insurance Building on the corner of La Salle and Adams Streets. That was in 1884. Six years later Jenney soared higher with his Manhattan Building, completely erected on a steel frame—all sixteen floors, at 431 South Dearborn.

14

NEWBERRY LIBRARY

At the same time, architect Henry Ives Cobb, co-designer of the overwhelmingly opulent Potter Palmer castle, was drawing up plans for the building named for its benefactor, pioneer merchant-banker Walter Loomis Newberry. With millions of books and manuscripts, with priceless map collections and an active program of exhibits and education, the Newberry Library is one of the most important research facilities in the country.

15

Major Jenney's office was a training ground for what would emerge as The Chicago School, and at the top of the class was Louis Sullivan who arrived to find the city "A crude extravaganza: An intoxicating rawness: A sense of big things to be done." With John Wellborn Root, Daniel Burnham and Dankmar Adler, he developed a form-follows-function philosophy, but in the process created Art Nouveau and, with Adler, designed one of the most extraordinarily beautiful buildings ever built—the Auditorium. President Harrison dedicated it in 1889 and Caruso, McCormick and Nellie Moore sang in its theater, the largest opera house in the world.

When the Monadnock Building
was being planned in 1891,
its builders were ridiculed for
choosing a site so far from the
city center, a site too near one
of the less reputable sections
of town. It was the heaviest
structure ever built, and the
last load-bearing wall
skyscraper. The days of the
lighter steel skeleton had
definitely arrived.

THE AUDITORIUM
AND THE STUDIO BUILDING

MONADNOCK BLOCK

17

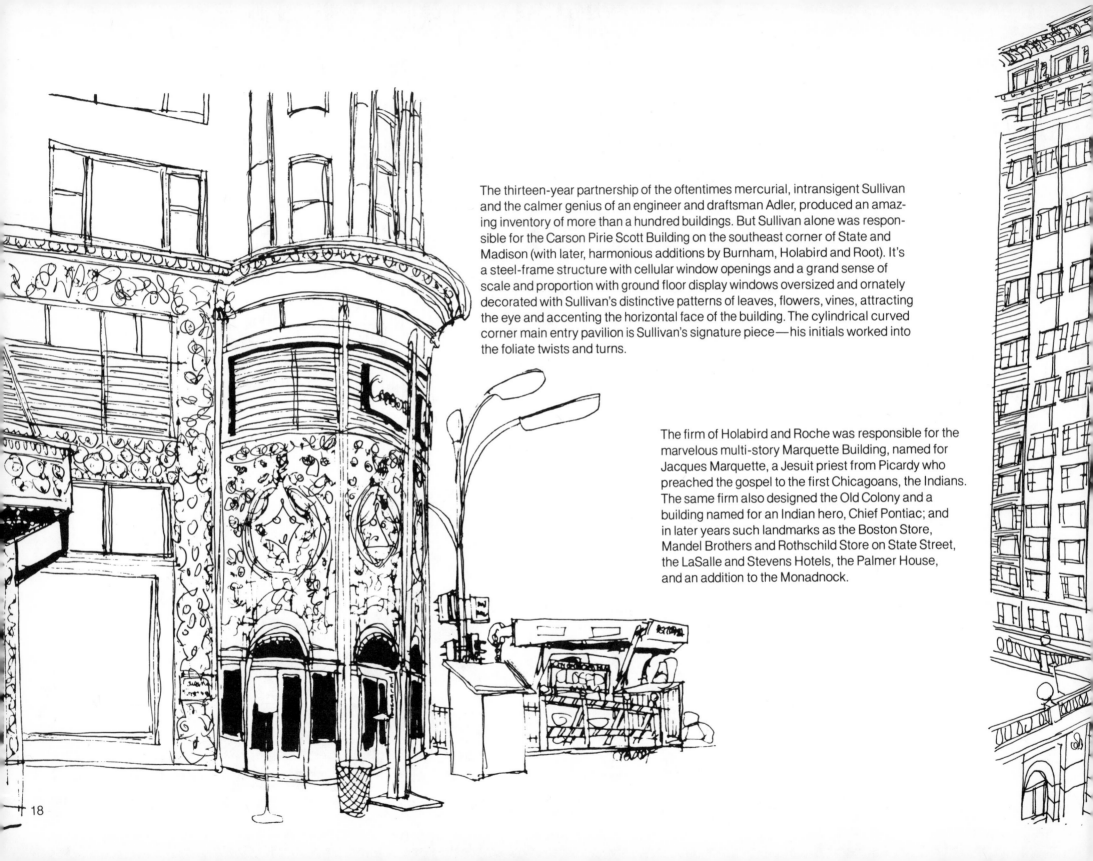

The thirteen-year partnership of the oftentimes mercurial, intransigent Sullivan and the calmer genius of an engineer and draftsman Adler, produced an amazing inventory of more than a hundred buildings. But Sullivan alone was responsible for the Carson Pirie Scott Building on the southeast corner of State and Madison (with later, harmonious additions by Burnham, Holabird and Root). It's a steel-frame structure with cellular window openings and a grand sense of scale and proportion with ground floor display windows oversized and ornately decorated with Sullivan's distinctive patterns of leaves, flowers, vines, attracting the eye and accenting the horizontal face of the building. The cylindrical curved corner main entry pavilion is Sullivan's signature piece—his initials worked into the foliate twists and turns.

The firm of Holabird and Roche was responsible for the marvelous multi-story Marquette Building, named for Jacques Marquette, a Jesuit priest from Picardy who preached the gospel to the first Chicagoans, the Indians. The same firm also designed the Old Colony and a building named for an Indian hero, Chief Pontiac; and in later years such landmarks as the Boston Store, Mandel Brothers and Rothschild Store on State Street, the LaSalle and Stevens Hotels, the Palmer House, and an addition to the Monadnock.

MARQUETTE BUILDING
1893-94

The Rookery, a Burnham and Root creations from the 1880s, was an Aladdin's castle for a little boy whose father, Carl Oscar Tolf, worked somewhere past the namesake rooks carved into the entrance, past the marble staircases and gloved, uniformed attendants, in the towers of Paine Webber—where for fifty-five years he was a stockbroker.

THE ROOKERY 1885

19

Frank Lloyd Wright, the foremost student of Sullivan (he called him "Lieber Meister," Beloved Master), remodeled the Rookery lobby in 1905 and later developed his own distinctive Prairie Style, viewing his buildings "primarily not as a cave but as a broad shelter in the open, related to vista, vista without and vista within."—as he wrote in his aptly titled *The Natural House.* His 1909 Robie House proves the point—horizontal and vertical lines in severely simple, layered cookie sheet patterns, with broad-shouldered roofs and boldly overhanging eaves.

ROBIE HOUSE
& U of C.

EMIL BACH HOUSE 7415 N. SHERIDAN RD
DESIGNED BY FRANK LLOYD WRIGHT. (1915)

His 1915 Emil Bach House confirms his rejection of extraneous add-ons, of curves, of anything
but lines as plane as the plain. For reenforcement of the concepts, plan a pilgrimage to Wright's
Oak Park, seven miles from downtown and like Chicago, a living museum of architecture.

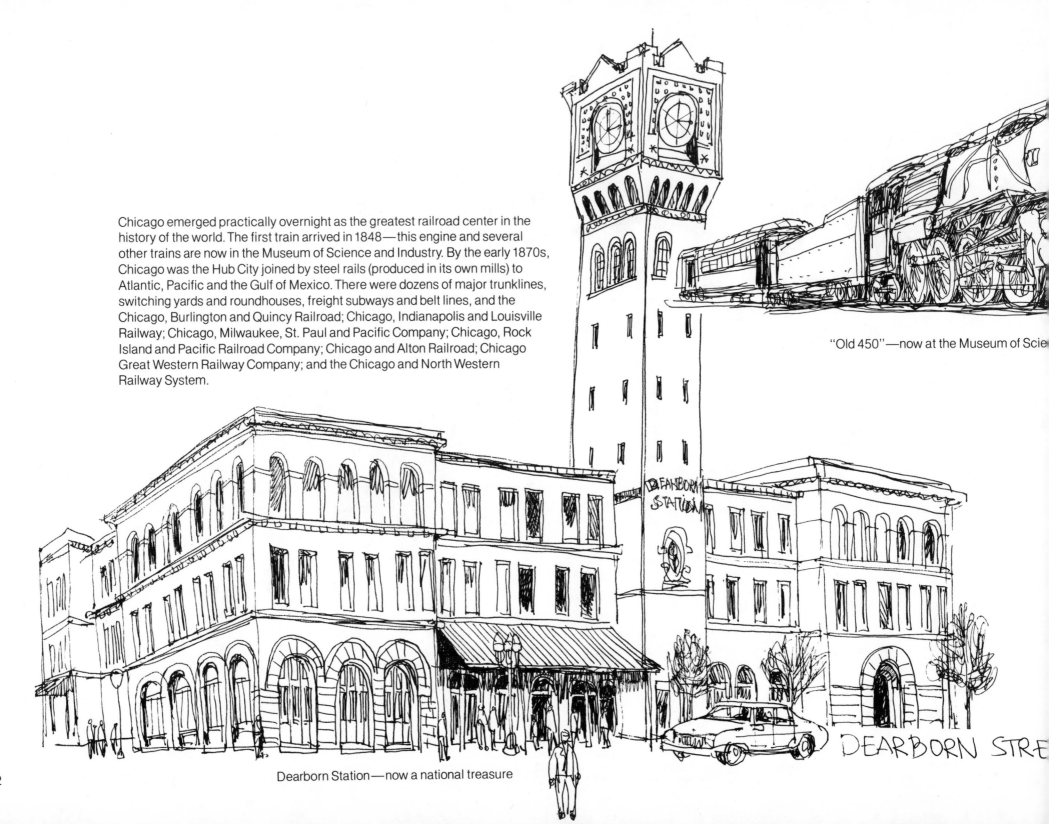

Chicago emerged practically overnight as the greatest railroad center in the history of the world. The first train arrived in 1848—this engine and several other trains are now in the Museum of Science and Industry. By the early 1870s, Chicago was the Hub City joined by steel rails (produced in its own mills) to Atlantic, Pacific and the Gulf of Mexico. There were dozens of major trunklines, switching yards and roundhouses, freight subways and belt lines, and the Chicago, Burlington and Quincy Railroad; Chicago, Indianapolis and Louisville Railway; Chicago, Milwaukee, St. Paul and Pacific Company; Chicago, Rock Island and Pacific Railroad Company; Chicago and Alton Railroad; Chicago Great Western Railway Company; and the Chicago and North Western Railway System.

"Old 450"—now at the Museum of Scie

Dearborn Station—now a national treasure

DEARBORN STRE

d Industry

UNION STATION

Anyone who was anybody going anywhere had to come through Chicago, and its railway stations were Mecca for Celebrity-watchers. Statesmen and sports legends, movie stars and impressarios, and the exiled royals, could be seen in Chicago stations — the Dearborn and Grand Central, the Union, LaSalle Street and North Western Stations. The Union Station survives, as well as the 1885 distinctively nostalgic Dearborn, though with truncated tower and without peaked roofs.

STATION

Care & Feeding of Mind & Soul

Schools, colleges, universities, research institutes and libraries, museums everywhere including African, Indian, Italian, Judaica, Lithuanian, Mexican, Polish, Romanian, Swedish and Ukranian, tributes to the fascinating ethnic mix of Chicago—that's the cultural side of a super city.

And churches large and small, old and new, dot the landscape, caring for the souls and spirit, reflecting that diversity, that democracy and freedom just as surely as the buildings themselves.

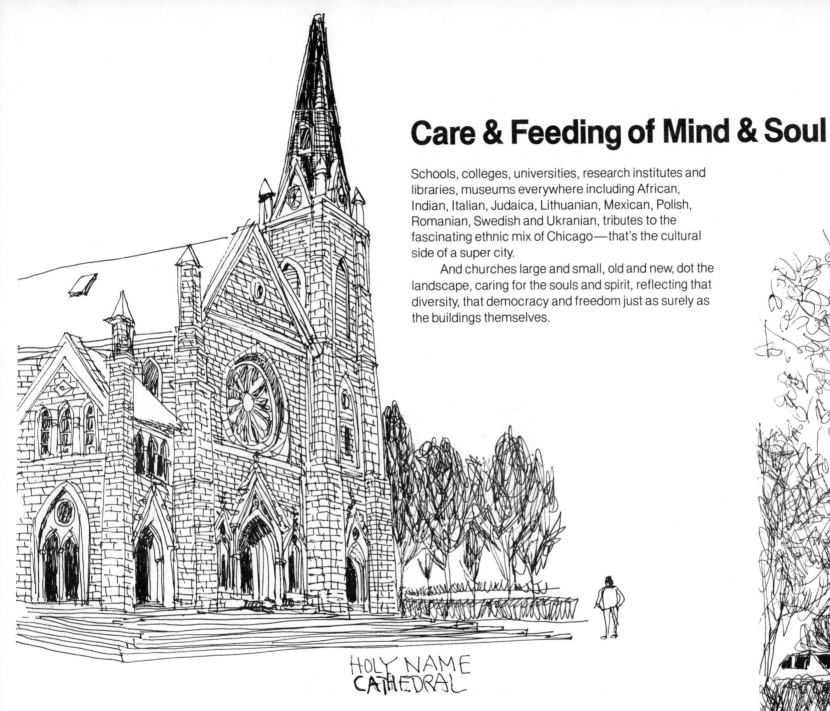

HOLY NAME
CATHEDRAL

Holy Name Cathedral, Chicago's testament to the middle ages, has served Chicago's Catholics for over a century and a half.

Integral and innovative adjuncts to the Art Institute are the Goodman Theatre, oldest established theater
in the city, and the
School of the Art Institute, internationally recognized as a college of art and design.

THE SCHOOL OF THE ART INSTITUTE OF CHICAGO

AT GOODMAN THEATRE

Founded in 1879, the Art Institute was moved to its lion-guarded Michigan Avenue home after the close of the 1893 Columbian Exposition. It was used for the World's Congresses during the fair, but was quickly converted to an art museum, one with incomparable collections of the French Impressionists, the Dutch Masters, American landscape painters and much, much more.

ART INSTITUTE FROM
THE CLIFFDWELLERS CLUB.

One of the world's largest—and finest—collections of ancient artifacts from the Near East is the University of Chicago's Oriental Institute. Its museum is a splendid showcase of the history, art and archaeology of the area, explored by the Institute-sponsored expeditions since 1919.

ORIENTAL INSTITUTE
UNIVERSITY OF CHICAGO

A Gothic memorial to the great benefactor of the University of Chicago, the Rockefeller Chapel was designed by the same architect, Bertram Goodhue, responsible for the Empire State Building. It is the repository of the ashes of the university presidents—and their wives—and its carillon has the second largest tuned bell in the world.

The DuSable Museum of African American History on 56th Place honors the memory of Chicago's first settler and houses an outstanding collection of African artifacts and material on Blacks in Chicago and Illinois history—the educational and publication programs make the museum a unique asset in the city.

DUSABLE MUSEUM OF AFRICAN AMERICAN HISTORY

29

Chicago's newest sparkler in the constellation of cultural stars is the Terra Museum of American Art, founded in 1980 and moved into its Michigan Avenue home seven years later. It's from the beneficience of Daniel J. Terra, modern-day entrepreneur and collector of major American art, including Samuel F. B. Morse's "The Gallery of the Louvre," purchased in 1982 for $3.2 million.

TERRA MUSEUM OF AMERICAN ART

Unheralded, and for years suffering from neglect, the Chicago Public Library has been reborn as the Cultural Center, its interior mosaics—some of the best and brightest in the country—cleaned and restored. And on the top floor is the Grand Army of the Republic Memorial Museum, a handsomely paneled hall with fine portraits and busts of Civil War leaders and generals who wore the blue—one of several reminders in town of the importance of that struggle to Chicago.

Marshall Field I financed the Field Museum of Natural History, founded in 1983 and initially housed in the Columbian Exposition Palace of Fine Arts Building (now the Museum of Science and Industry)—he got it going with a million dollar bequest and then left it another eight million in his will. By that time the incredible collections portraying the natural history of man and his earth were in this eleven-acre Greek temple, with awesome fighting bull elephants dominating center stage of the main floor, with overwhelming skeletons of whales and pre-historic brontosaurus and gorgosaurus, with Egyptian mummies and the world's largest exhibit of three-dimensional plants—only a few of the more than thirteen million items in the inventory.

CHICAGO CULTURAL CENTER

FIELD MUSEUM
WITH CHICAGO SKYLINE

31

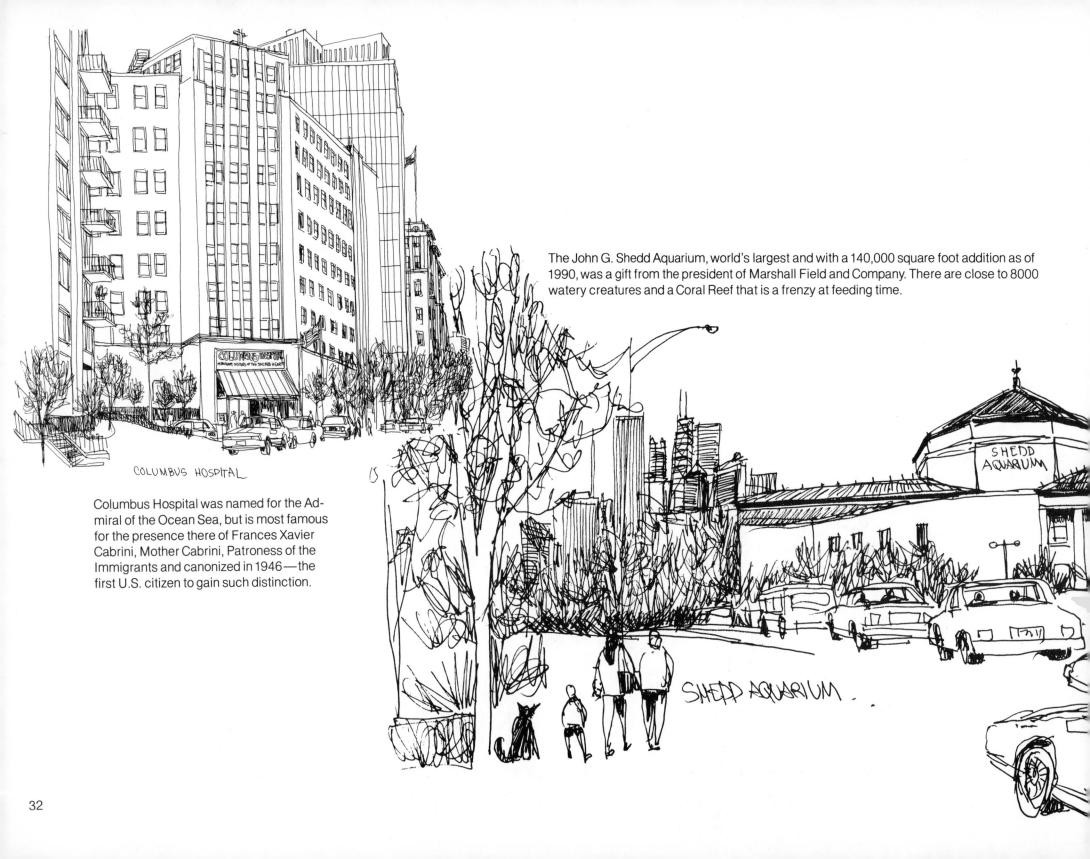

The John G. Shedd Aquarium, world's largest and with a 140,000 square foot addition as of 1990, was a gift from the president of Marshall Field and Company. There are close to 8000 watery creatures and a Coral Reef that is a frenzy at feeding time.

COLUMBUS HOSPITAL

Columbus Hospital was named for the Admiral of the Ocean Sea, but is most famous for the presence there of Frances Xavier Cabrini, Mother Cabrini, Patroness of the Immigrants and canonized in 1946—the first U.S. citizen to gain such distinction.

SHEDD AQUARIUM.

NORTHWESTERN UNIVERSITY
CHICAGO CAMPUS.

Northwestern University is located in suburban Evanston, but has a huge graduate school
Chicago campus as well, a merger of collegiate Gothic with more modern expressions.

33

The Tree Studios on State and Ontario Streets, in the shadow of the Medinah Temple, were built to house Chicago artists, and early on they were home to the rebels against the classicists and traditionalists. Today, there are forty artists in residence, including Bill Olendorf, Marya Lillien, head of the Frank Lloyd Wright Foundation, and Jim Romano, designer and artist who resides in the former studio of J. A. St. John, the original illustrator of Tarzan for Edgar Rice Burrows.

TREE STUDIOS
STATE & ONTARIO

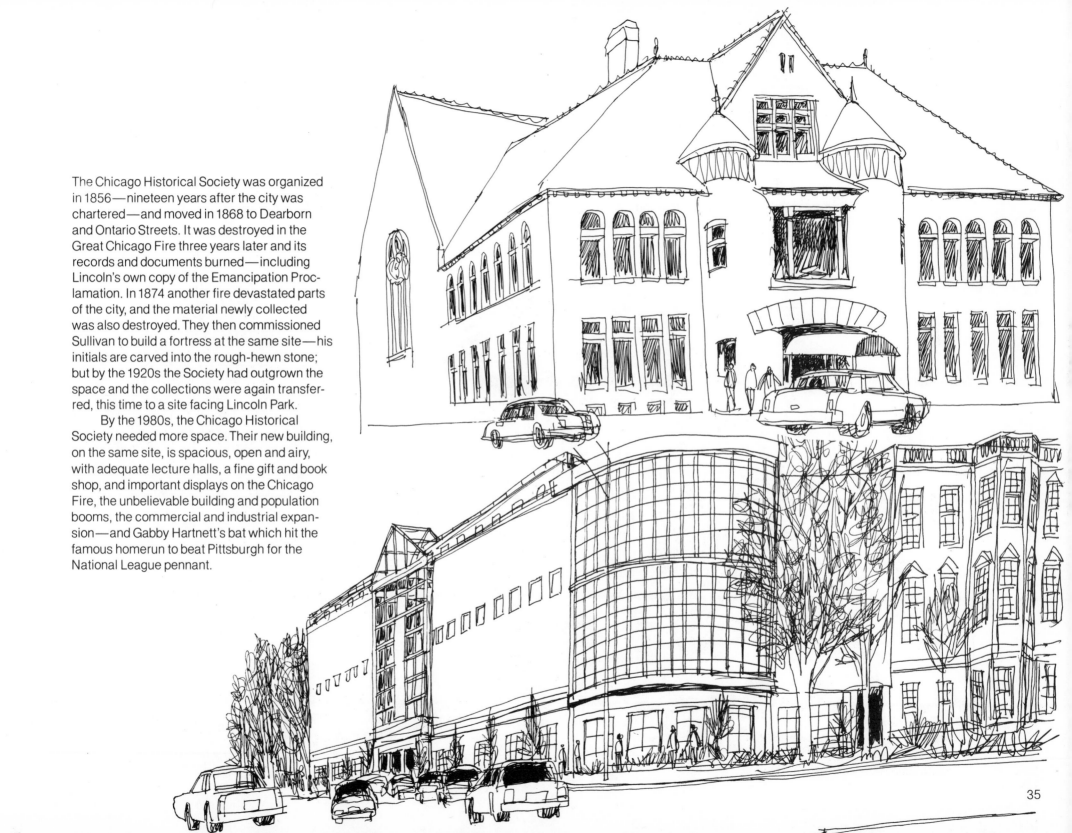

The Chicago Historical Society was organized in 1856—nineteen years after the city was chartered—and moved in 1868 to Dearborn and Ontario Streets. It was destroyed in the Great Chicago Fire three years later and its records and documents burned—including Lincoln's own copy of the Emancipation Proclamation. In 1874 another fire devastated parts of the city, and the material newly collected was also destroyed. They then commissioned Sullivan to build a fortress at the same site—his initials are carved into the rough-hewn stone; but by the 1920s the Society had outgrown the space and the collections were again transferred, this time to a site facing Lincoln Park.

By the 1980s, the Chicago Historical Society needed more space. Their new building, on the same site, is spacious, open and airy, with adequate lecture halls, a fine gift and book shop, and important displays on the Chicago Fire, the unbelievable building and population booms, the commercial and industrial expansion—and Gabby Hartnett's bat which hit the famous homerun to beat Pittsburgh for the National League pennant.

The year after the Chicago Historical Society was founded, the Chicago Academy of Sciences was organized—the oldest science museum in the Midwest. Here you can go way, way back, to walk-through exhibits of Chicago 300 million years ago, and then visit the natural flora and fauna of the area.

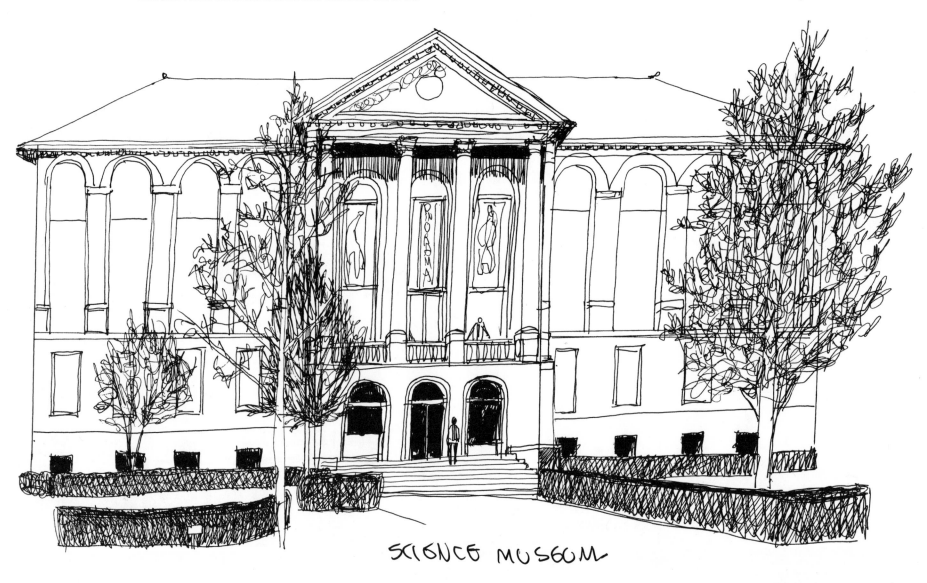

SCIENCE MUSEUM

IIT, the Illinois Institute of Technology, was established in 1940 with the merger of the 1896 Lewis Institute. The hundred-acre campus has some twenty buildings by that German Bauhaus master of clean angularity and rigorous linear motif, Ludwig Mies van der Rohe. Focal point of the South State Street campus is the S. R. Crown Hall, pavilion of glass and black steel that served as headquarters for Mies, director of the IIT School of Architecture.

ILLINOIS INSTITUTE OF TECHNOLOGY

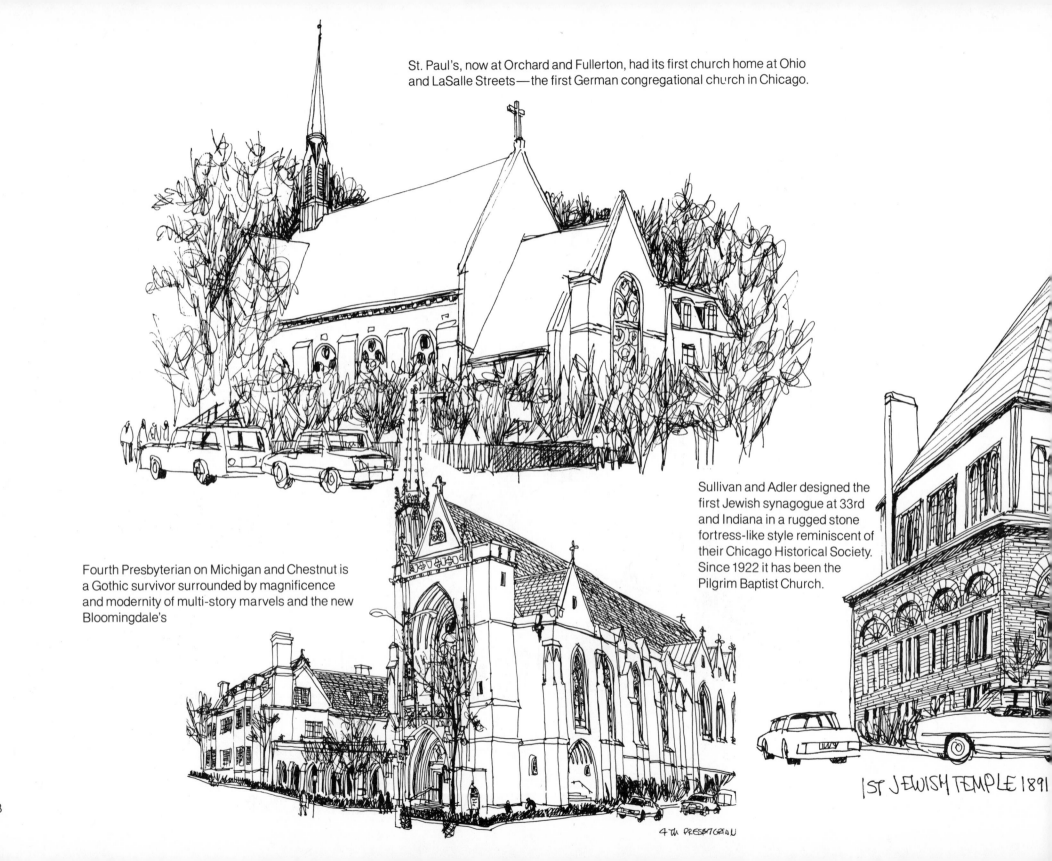

St. Paul's, now at Orchard and Fullerton, had its first church home at Ohio and LaSalle Streets—the first German congregational church in Chicago.

Sullivan and Adler designed the first Jewish synagogue at 33rd and Indiana in a rugged stone fortress-like style reminiscent of their Chicago Historical Society. Since 1922 it has been the Pilgrim Baptist Church.

Fourth Presbyterian on Michigan and Chestnut is a Gothic survivor surrounded by magnificence and modernity of multi-story marvels and the new Bloomingdale's

4TH PRESBYTERIAN

1ST JEWISH TEMPLE 1891

FIRST BAPTIST CONGREGATIONAL CHURCH 1869.
60 N. ASHLAND AVE.

The First Baptist Congregational Church at Washington and Ashland was built in 1869 and survived the Great Fire.

PILGRIM BAPTIST CHURCH

St. James, at Wabash and Huron, is the Cathedral Church of the Episcopalians and for years was distinguished by the presence on the staff of famed organist Leo Sowerby.

St JAMES CATHEDRAL

Louis Sullivan was commissioned in 1903 to create, at 1121 North Leavitt, an encapsulation of Orthodox Russian provincial church architecture, and he was so eager for the challenge that he did the designing for half the usual commission of ten percent. Of the three religious structures he planned, only this expression of genius, the Holy Trinity Russian Orthodox Cathedral, survived as he intended, a sublime synthesis.

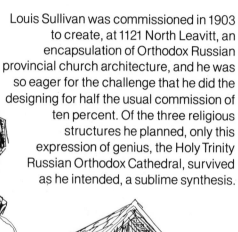

HOLY TRINITY CATHEDRAL
1903 LOUIS SULLIVAN
ARCHITECT

Built in 1881, the Assumption Catholic Church of the Servite Fathers continues to flourish in the shadow of the soaring skyscrapers. Mother Cabrini opened the day school in 1899.

41

Cocoon of Creativity

There is another Chicago School every bit as dynamic, democratic and tradition-smashing as the architects. It is the school in which Theodore Dreiser, Upton Sinclair, Frank Norris, Edna Ferber, Edgar Lee Masters, Vachel Lindsay, James T. Farrell, Meyer Levin, Thornton Wilder, Sherwood Anderson, Nelson Algren and Saul Bellow were the faculty. No wonder H. L. Mencken called Chicago "the only genuinely civilized city in the New World."

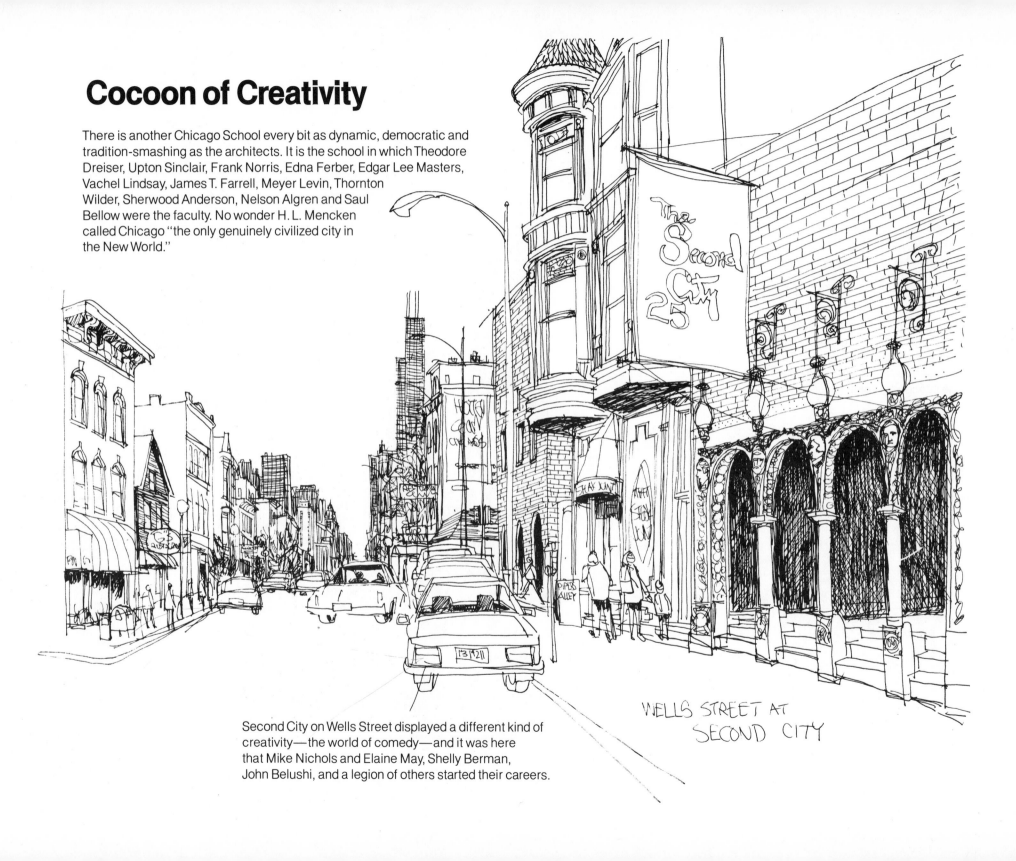

WELLS STREET AT SECOND CITY

Second City on Wells Street displayed a different kind of creativity—the world of comedy—and it was here that Mike Nichols and Elaine May, Shelly Berman, John Belushi, and a legion of others started their careers.

There was also the Chicago School of Journalism, and the deans were Carl Sandburg and Ben Hecht, author with Charles MacArthur of a classic on the subject, *The Front Page.* Ring Lardner and Westbrook Pegler were sports writers, and Eugene Field, when he wasn't writing children's poetry ("Wynken, Blynken and Nod"), a columnist with the likes of the unique political humorist Finley Peter Dunne, whose "Mr. Dooley" has never been duplicated.

CHICAGO DAILY NEWS BUILDING
1989

In the fastness of the soaring tower of the powerful *Chicago Tribune,* there were such brilliant book editors as Burton Fascoe and Bob Cromie, and the one-of-a-kind Colonel Robert R. McCormick, whose education and experience led him to the conclusion that "when real American culture and tradition have become native to the mind of a more homogenous and better-fused people, the position of Chicago as the national capital of the country will become an axiom."

After his World War II career on the "Stars & Stripes" where he created "G-I Joe", Bill Maulden lived and worked in the second low-rise studio at LaSalle and Goethe in Sandburg Village.

The home of one of Chicago's great painters ("The Picture of Dorian Gray"), Ivan Albright, on Division Street near Lake Shore Drive.

ESSANAY STUDIOS

The Essanay Studios on Argyle, said by many to be the original home of film comedy, thrived for several years in an unpopulated area on Chicago's north side. It is where Charlie Chaplin, the Marx Brothers, Lillian Gish, Wallace Berry and many other silent film stars made their first movies.

And they lived in these modest company-owned quarters, the Essanay Apartments, across the street.

John Barrymore called this three-story frame house his home for one year late in his career. in Old Town on Eugenie Street.

ESSANAY APARTMENTS

47

The home and studio of Chicago's world-class fashion photographer,
Victor Skrebneski on North LaSalle Street.

DEARBORN PK U

48

In this townhouse on North Dearborn Parkway, a young Ernest Hemingway, fresh from the war, just married, wrote about his summers in Michigan, and dreamed about going to Paris.

In a far different literary vein, another up-and-coming Chicagoan, Hugh Hefner, was producing in a couple of rooms at this Superior Street address the first issues of *Playboy*.

FIRST HOME OF PLAYBOY MAGAZINE

Where Fortunes Are Made and Sometimes Lost

THE GREAT TRADING FLOOR OF THE CHICAGO MERCANTILE EXCHANGE, LARGEST FINANCIAL FUTURES MARKET IN THE WORLD.

One Financial Place is a 1985 forty-story triumph of the Skidmore, Owings & Merrill firm, worthy successors to Sullivan-Burnham-Root-Adler. Flanked by the Midwest Stock Exchange to the south and the Chicago Board Options Exchange to the north, the red granite, bronze-tinted glass building stands on the site once occupied by the LaSalle Street Station and once owned by Bill Olendorf's great-great grandfather—he traded the land for a wagon.

The new Chicago Mercantile Exchange on South Wacker Drive races along the river in a block-long complex flanked by a pair of forty-story towers with a series of serrated edges permitting sixteen corner offices per floor. The Three-story center is the focal point, with 40,000 square feet of unimpeded trading floor (with another 30,000 upstairs as spare) where everything from pork bellies and livestock to Italian lira and T-bills are traded.

53

This is the world's largest trading pit at The Chicago Board Options Exchange, a beehive of bustling activity, a High Tech colossus of financial communications.

The always-hushed canyon of LaSalle Street, with its banks and financial institutions, is watched over by the statue of Ceres, Goddess of Grain and Harvest, high atop the symetrically soaring Board of Trade Building, tallest in the city when completed in 1930, and an Art Deco masterpiece by Holabird and Root, two of the most important architects of the Chicago School. Founded in 1848, the Board of Trade has played a key role in the development of the city—and the Tolf family: grandfather Axel Frederick Tolf was a member, in the firm of Robert Lindblom, a prominent Swedish sucess story; and brother Carl Oscar Tolf was once a runner to the wheat pit. Harry Olendorf, father of the artist Bill Olendorf, after his return from World War I, was the youngest trader on the floor of the old Board of Trade.

CHICAGO BOARD OF TRADE 55

The mighty legs of the First National Bank are planted solidly in the center of the financial district with the Third National Center.

56

Designed by the successor firm to Daniel Burnham, and completed the same year as the Board of Trade, the Merchandise Mart is another landmark on Chicago's "largest" list—the world's largest office building. Its surprising next door neighbor is Helene Curtis Co. in a new rehabbed world headquarters building.

MERCHANDISE MART
HELENE CURTIS BLDG
& CRIBBONS SEXTITW
BLDG.

57

In the strange bedfellows category of notable Chicago homes is this gabled four-story built at the turn of the century, and decades later transformed into a bunny hutch—Playboy Mansion. Now it's used as a dormitory by its new owners, the Art Institute.

PLAYBOY MANSION N.STATE PARKWAY.

These Walls Talk

It was a favorite expression of Carl Sandburg, and there's surely no shortage of talking walls in Chicago, of structures to trigger memory banks and set fire to the imagination.

WRIGLEY HOUSE

Chewing gum magnate Wrigley certainly did not win all the games with his Chicago Cubs, nor with his wife. When he insisted they build this mansion mid-north, facing Lincoln Park away from the social excitement of the day, she spent minimum time in it.

STATE & RANDOLPH

"Meet me at the clock!" are Chicago buzzwords
for Marshall Field's green filigree finger holding up the time at the corner of State and Randolph.

Why is the Loop called the Loop? Take a ride on the L, the elevated rapid transit, and stick with it while it loops its way to box in the heart of downtown.

WABASH AVENUE AT MONROE ST.

One of the most beautiful homes in all of modern Chicago is this posh penthouse on top of a Lake Shore Drive skyscraper overlooking all of the city and the lake. Called "The Castle in the Sky" its original owner—George Woodruff—was related to the Morton Salt fortune.

On tree-shaded Astor Street, this classic Louis XVI creation by David Adler in 1921 was for the Ryerson family. Family fortunes go back to 1842 when the first Ryerson started a company in Chicago that would eventually evolve into Inland Steel.

RYERSON HOME – ASTOR STREET

The Union Stock Yards covered hundreds of acres between Ashland and Halsted and were home, briefly, for millions and millions of animals manhandled and processed by thousands and thousands of workers. Meat-packing was the most important and most characteristic industry for the hog butcher of the world, and the princes of packingtown prospered greatly—the Armours, Morrises, Swifts. Closed in 1971, all that remains today is the main gate.

STOCK YARDS

In 1889, a local promoter—William H. Grey—decided to do something completely different: import brick by brick the entire Libby Prison, an infamous Civil War leftover in Richmond. The bricks were then mortared into the front façade of the Coliseum, which had its own notoriety—it's where those models of big city boodle, Bathhouse John and Hinky Dink Kenna, held their political rallies—meaning let-it-all-hang-out parties, if not orgies. If you want to see the bricks today, look for the last remaining chunks of wall at South Wabash and 14th Street.

Right: House of William Hauser Grey on Dearborn Parkway built in 1884.

ALL THATS LEFT - LIBBY PRISON
SOUTH WABASH AVE.

Left: The Cuneo Castle on North State Street has its own kind of inner-city chateau charm and was an in-town retreat for the millionaire printer before he sought greener pastures out in horse country, where he took over and greatly improved and added to the Samuel Insull estate.

1364 N. STATE

Above: This powerful statement on the corner of Wabash and Erie Streets has a lavishly designed interior filled with museum-caliber carved wood and marble, marble everywhere. It was built in 1883 for Samuel M. Nickerson, a New Englander who arrived in the city just before the Civil War with the suit on his back and some loose change. He prospered mightily and was one of the founders and then president of the First National Bank. Today it is owned by the American College of Surgeons and Nickerson's Marble Palace serves as their reception rooms.

The high rises get
closer and have taken over
such treasures as the home
of Chicago School architect, John
Wellborn Root; but, shaded by trees and
introduced by carefully manicured patches
of greenery, the survivors hang on, exuding an air of quiet affluence.

ASTOR STREET

Remembrance of Past & Present

It used to be said that the only time Chicago bows to history is when it has to make the bend on Michigan Avenue when it goes past the old Water Tower. Nonsense! Chicago does not make a fetish out of it, but the past is respected—and honored and protected and preserved in many of its parts. All the while remembering that it alone produced A Century of Progress, that Chicago has always looked to its tomorrows, while building on its past.

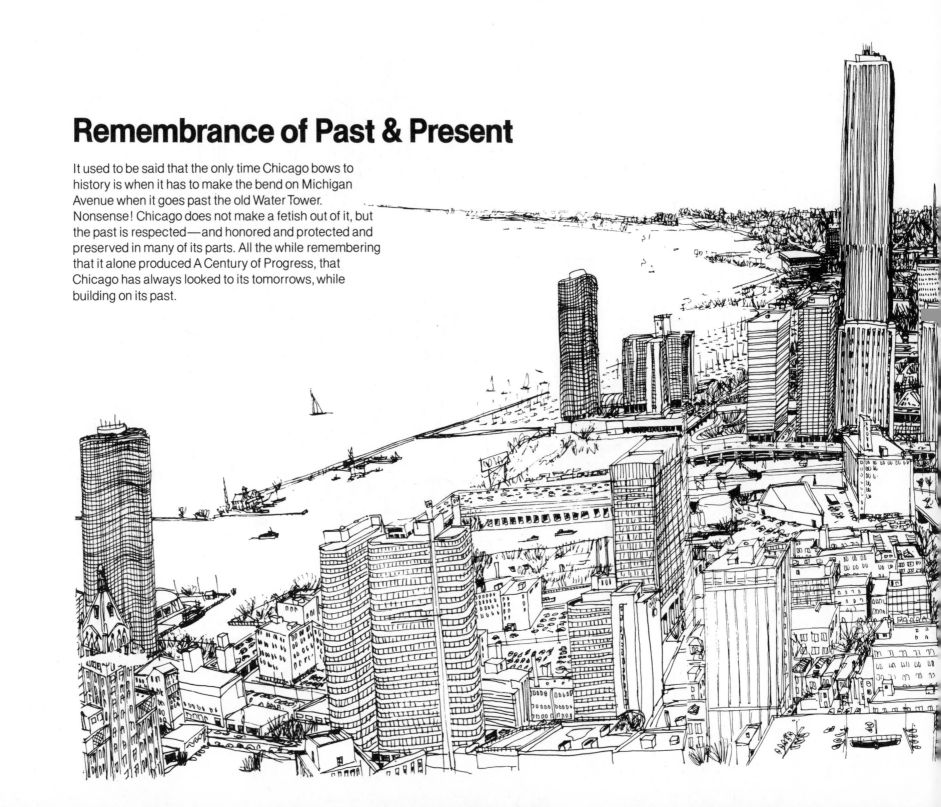

What better proof of combining the best of two possible worlds, of yesterday and today, than the placement of this 1890 fountain on Wacker Drive, along the river in the middle of so much modernity.

ELKS MEMORIAL.

Or building a world-class memorial to the Benevolent and Patriotic Order of Elks, founded in 1969 and still headquartered in Chicago.

Or planting a remarkable Henry Moore sculpture precisely on the place where, underneath the west grandstand of Stagg Field at the University of Chicago, the modern age of man began, when on December 2, 1942, the secret of the atom was unlocked.

UNIVERSITY OF CHICAGO - SITE OF FIRST SELF-SUSTAINED NUCLEAR CHAIN REACTION 1942

HENRY MOORE SCULPTURE -

71

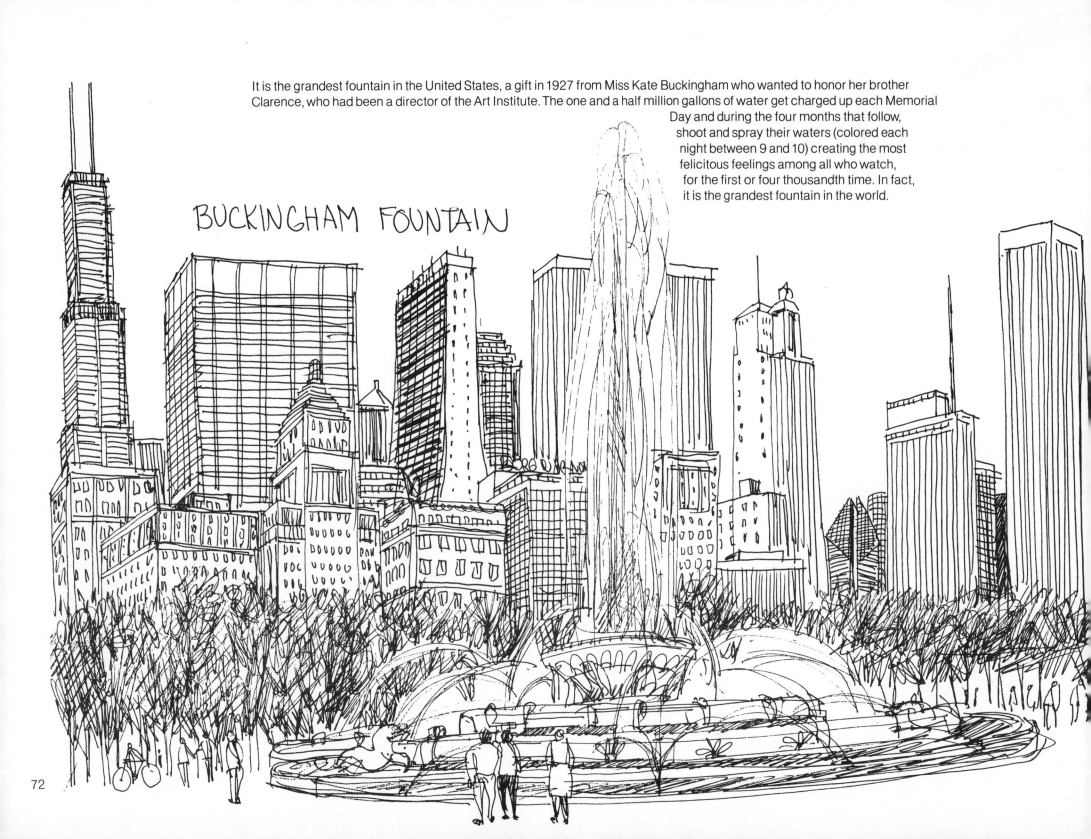

It is the grandest fountain in the United States, a gift in 1927 from Miss Kate Buckingham who wanted to honor her brother Clarence, who had been a director of the Art Institute. The one and a half million gallons of water get charged up each Memorial Day and during the four months that follow, shoot and spray their waters (colored each night between 9 and 10) creating the most felicitous feelings among all who watch, for the first or four thousandth time. In fact, it is the grandest fountain in the world.

BUCKINGHAM FOUNTAIN

Joan Miro's "Mystery", a welcome newcomer, rising up 36 feet from Brunswick Plaza at the Civic Center, was lowered into place in April 1981—some say, to stare at the Picasso across the way in Daley Plaza.

THE MIRÓ
AT THE CIVIC CENTER

73

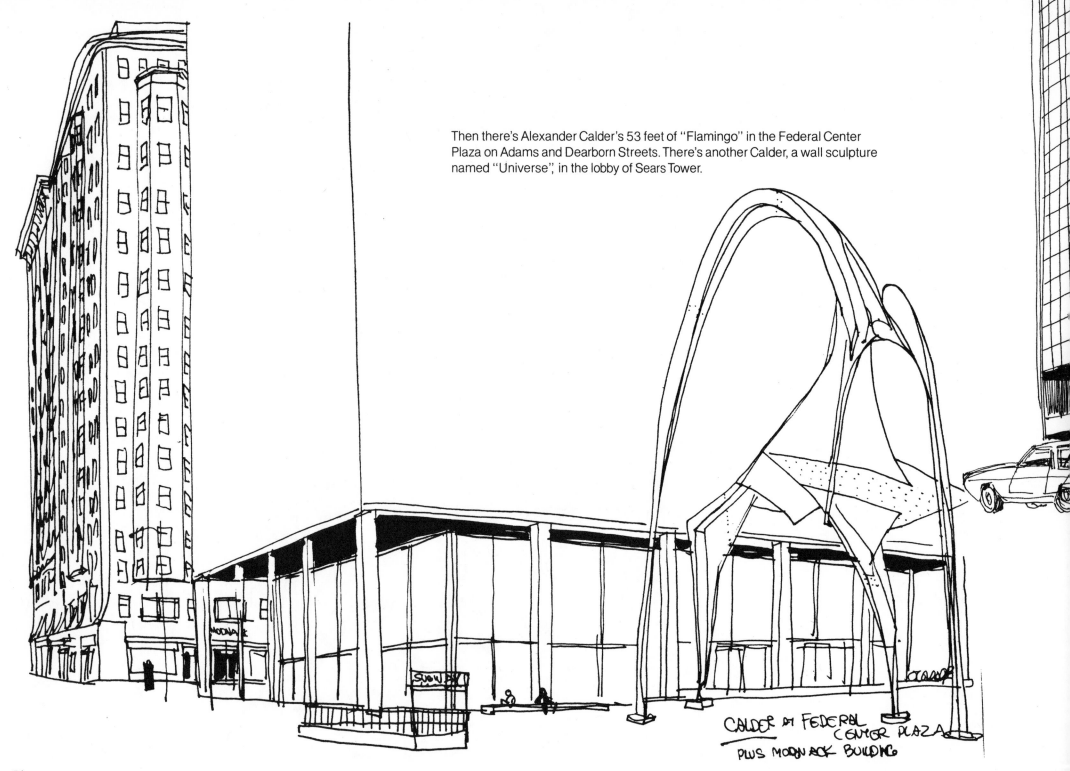

Then there's Alexander Calder's 53 feet of "Flamingo" in the Federal Center Plaza on Adams and Dearborn Streets. There's another Calder, a wall sculpture named "Universe", in the lobby of Sears Tower.

CALDER AT FEDERAL CENTER PLAZA
PLUS MONADNOCK BUILDING

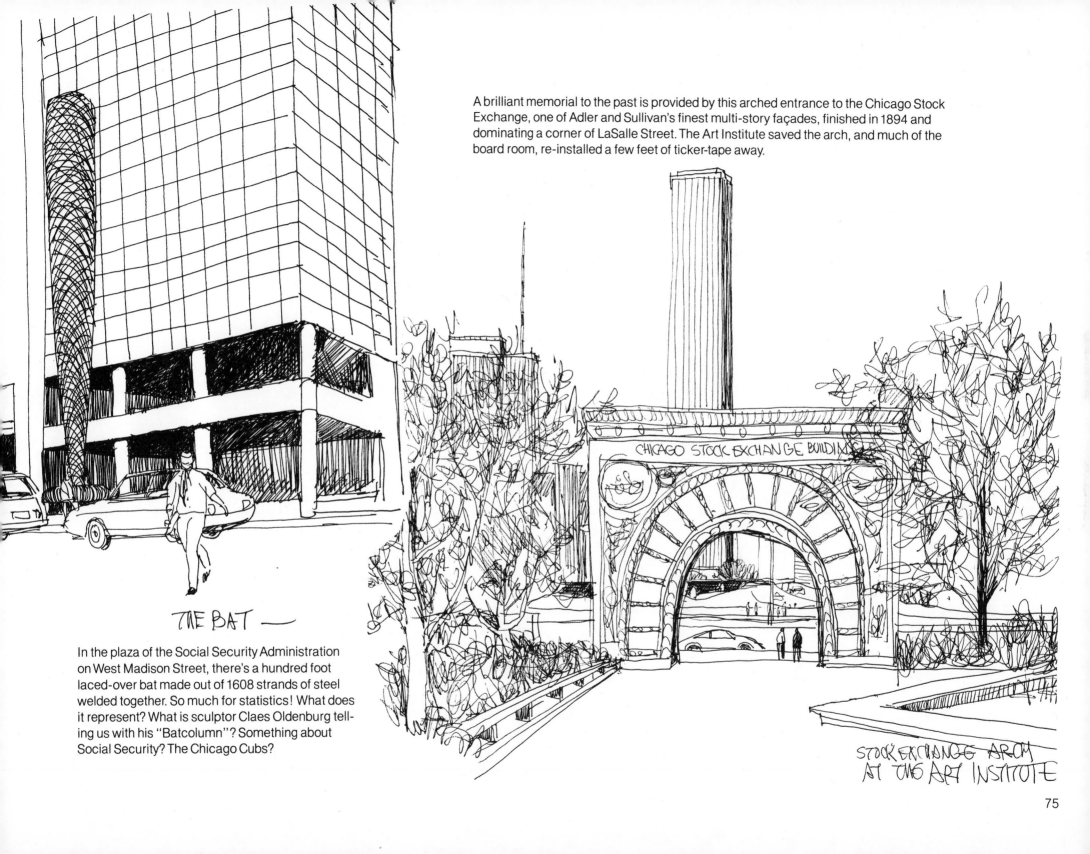

A brilliant memorial to the past is provided by this arched entrance to the Chicago Stock Exchange, one of Adler and Sullivan's finest multi-story façades, finished in 1894 and dominating a corner of LaSalle Street. The Art Institute saved the arch, and much of the board room, re-installed a few feet of ticker-tape away.

THE BAT —

In the plaza of the Social Security Administration on West Madison Street, there's a hundred foot laced-over bat made out of 1608 strands of steel welded together. So much for statistics! What does it represent? What is sculptor Claes Oldenburg telling us with his "Batcolumn"? Something about Social Security? The Chicago Cubs?

CHICAGO STOCK EXCHANGE BUILDING

STOCK EXCHANGE ARCH
AT THE ART INSTITUTE

The Fort Dearborn pioneers are memorialized by four super-size sculptures at the Michigan Avenue Bridge. This one faces south showing pioneers going forward.

Below: This neoclassical auditorium on Erie Street, next door to Nickerson's Marble Palace, was dedicated in 1926 "to advancement of surgery along its scientific and moral side." Its bronze doors are Chicago's answer to Ghiberti's sculpted masterworks on the Baptistry in Florence, and they depict the great heroes of medicine from Aesculapius to Lister, Osler and Pasteur.

DALEY PLAZA

Fifty feet of abstract steel was given to the city by Picasso in 1967 and it's been talked about ever since—although the kids love to climb on it, and maybe that's what Pablo intended.

Pioneer Court, honoring the shakers
and movers of the past with water
and stone. It was the site of the first
International Harvester plant.

PIONEER COURT

One of the several McCormick family mansions which have survived this one at Erie and Wabash Streets.

Below: The main thoroughfare leading to the great South Side, Martin Luther King, Jr. Drive.

Jean Dubuffet's "Monument with Standing Beast" provokes as much discussion as the State of Illinois Center, but in the world of art and Chicago architecture, what else is new?

In the First National Plaza at Monroe and Dearborn Streets, the Art in the City activists have installed seventy feet of glass and granite, marble and stone wall mural by Marc Chagall—he entitled it "The Four Seasons."

81

Water Water Everywhere

Long before the railroads, the turnpikes and the world's busiest airport, this heart of the heartlands owed it all to the water. The unparalleled explosion of commerce, trade and industry was predicated in its free-flowing abundance. First there is the great lake, then the river and its tributaries, the man-made canals, inlets, bridges and such safe harbors as the one named for Daniel Hudson Burnham, the visionary whose 1909 Plan of Chicago embraced the water and a series of parks, harbors and beaches for the people forevermore, with sure knowledge and sensitive spirit.

In 1833, Congress appropriated $25,000 for the dredging of the Chicago River, the clearing of sand bars blocking its mouth. Three years later, digging began on the Illinois and Michigan Canal (completed a dozen years later) and the entire village celebrated the even. A half century later the Sanitary and Ship Canal was opened, and in 1933 the Illinois Waterway. But the most dramatic development—in vintage Chicago-style—was the reversal of the flow of their river. and then the energetic engineers decided to straighten out that flow from lake downstream. Between 18th and 19th Streets they took out the bend.

The Chicago River at the Merchandise Mart and 333 West Wacker Drive

River Vista

The Coast Guard Station at the mouth of the river hangs in there braced by a background of Goliath sentinels.

And not far distant is the Chicago Yacht Club, home of the famous fleet which makes the annual race up Lake Michigan to Mackinac Island.

CHICAGO YACHT CLUB

MONROE STREET

TOP GALLANT
CHICAGO

Navy Pier, christened Municipal Pier when it was built in 1914–1916, was an integral part of the Burnham Plan of Chicago, and it stretched 3000 feet into the lake, designed to handle passenger and freight ships. It had its own streetcar tracks, recreational areas, and cavernous internal spaces which served as a wartime Naval Training Center, and then as a post-war college campus.

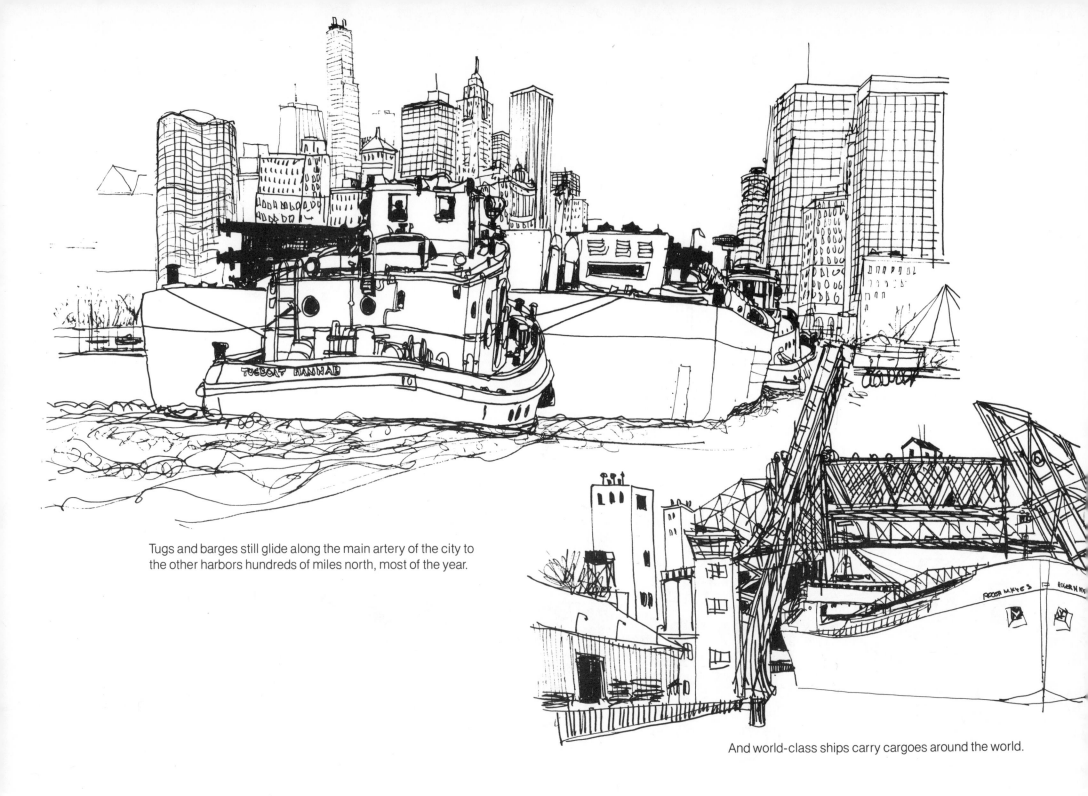

Tugs and barges still glide along the main artery of the city to the other harbors hundreds of miles north, most of the year.

And world-class ships carry cargoes around the world.

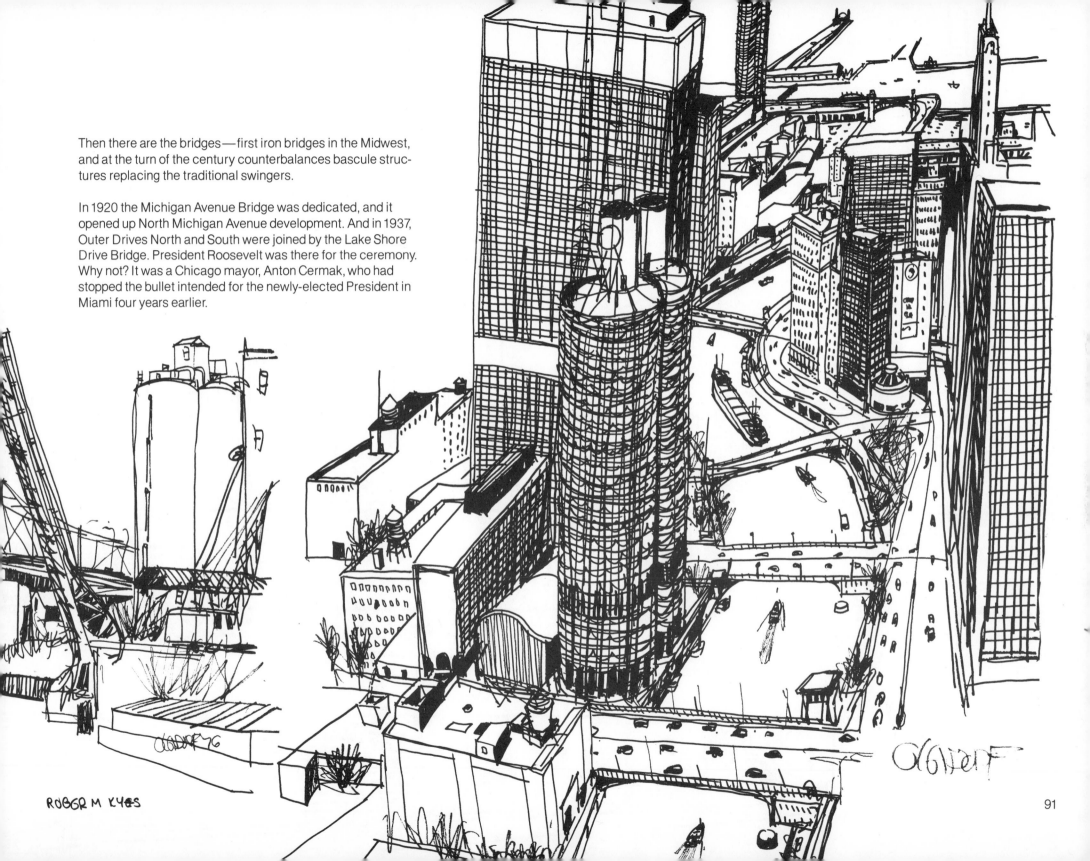

Then there are the bridges—first iron bridges in the Midwest, and at the turn of the century counterbalances bascule structures replacing the traditional swingers.

In 1920 the Michigan Avenue Bridge was dedicated, and it opened up North Michigan Avenue development. And in 1937, Outer Drives North and South were joined by the Lake Shore Drive Bridge. President Roosevelt was there for the ceremony. Why not? It was a Chicago mayor, Anton Cermak, who had stopped the bullet intended for the newly-elected President in Miami four years earlier.

ROBGR M KYGS

92

THE FLEET'S IN!

Not by Bread Alone

In Chicago man lives by excesses of ethnic exotics, superior steaks, expense account indulgences, ensconced in heaps of history, a fair share of nostalgia, and the inevitable trend-setters. Chicago is a major eating capital of the world.

Left: Butch McGuire's at 20 West Division started one of those trends—the uptown singles bar—but he's done so much more, in recruiting a smiling staff, many of them just off the boat from Ireland, and installing a competent kitchen producing fine omelets, beautiful burgers, sensational roast pork sandwiches and one-of-a-kind Irish whiskey loaf.

Right: Gene and Georgetti's, 500 North Franklin, a vibrant leftover from speakeasy days, is convenient to the Merchandise Mart, and features great linguine with white sauce, super spaghetti selections, palate-stimulating lobster diavolo and terrific garlic-rubbed steaks.

GENE & GEORGETTIS

RICCARDO'S RESTAURANT

BILLY

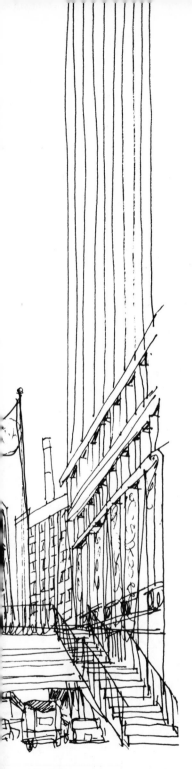

Left: Riccardo's is as much an institution as any restaurant in town since the 30s. A gathering place of artists, actors and writers who tell about their latest commission or conquest. Still the best spaghetti in Chicago!

Left: Billy Goat Tavern in a subterranean location, famous for the owner who kept his pet goat on the premises. Then John Belushi came along and was inspired to do the "Cheeseburgli, Cheeseburgli" routine on Saturday Night Live.

Right: The Bakery, 2218 North Lincoln Avenue, has been packing 'em in ever since it served its first currant-kissed beef Wellington in 1963. It's the domain of the unique, high-profile chef-owner Louis Szathmary who ranges world wide in his various promotions.

T TAVERN

THE BAKERY

97

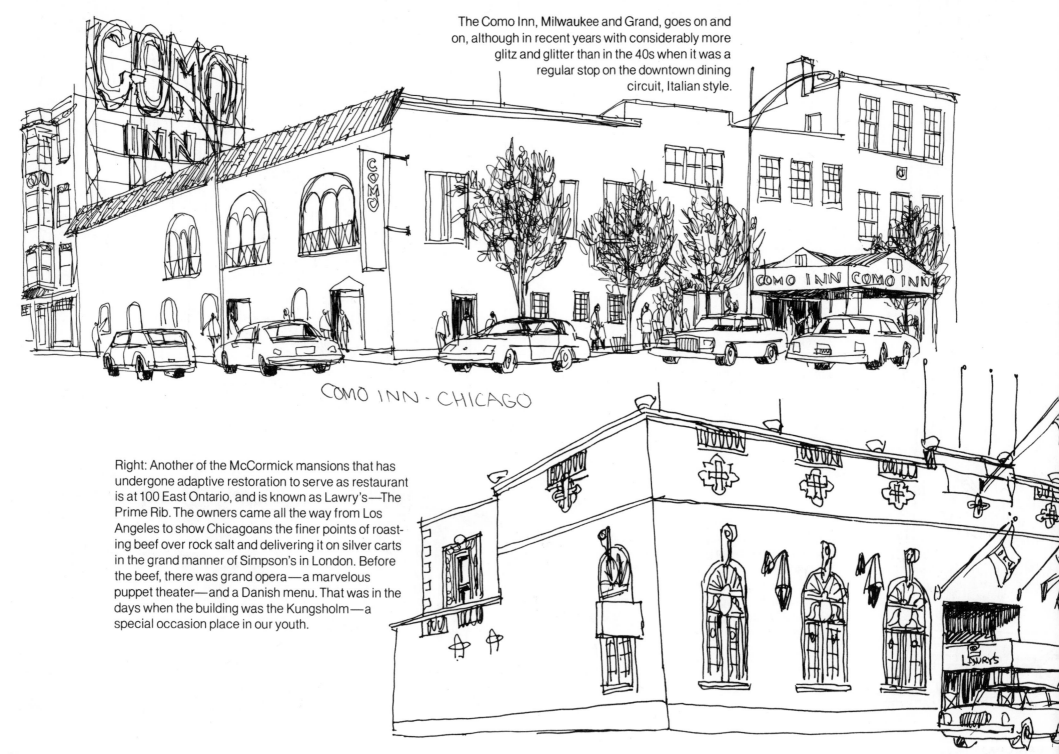

The Como Inn, Milwaukee and Grand, goes on and on, although in recent years with considerably more glitz and glitter than in the 40s when it was a regular stop on the downtown dining circuit, Italian style.

COMO INN - CHICAGO

Right: Another of the McCormick mansions that has undergone adaptive restoration to serve as restaurant is at 100 East Ontario, and is known as Lawry's—The Prime Rib. The owners came all the way from Los Angeles to show Chicagoans the finer points of roasting beef over rock salt and delivering it on silver carts in the grand manner of Simpson's in London. Before the beef, there was grand opera—a marvelous puppet theater—and a Danish menu. That was in the days when the building was the Kungsholm—a special occasion place in our youth.

Left: Chez Paul, French cuisine in a delightful setting, 660 Rush Street, was originally the home of R. Hall McCormick, a leading figure in the McCormick Harvesting Machine Company, and noted art collector. The mansion was finished in 1875 and was one of the group of McCormick mansions within a two-block radius.

CHEZ PAUL

Right: The Chicago Chop House at 60 West Ontario, is a newcomer, one that helps Chicagoans get over the demise of Mr. Kelly's, the Stockyard Inn and London House. The lamb chops are champions, and the steaks all prime and dry-aged a minimum of three weeks. It's a crash course in Chicago history, with photo portraits of all the mayors, grand old street shots and a rogues' gallery of gangsters going back to the beginning, when Chicago was a raw frontier town.

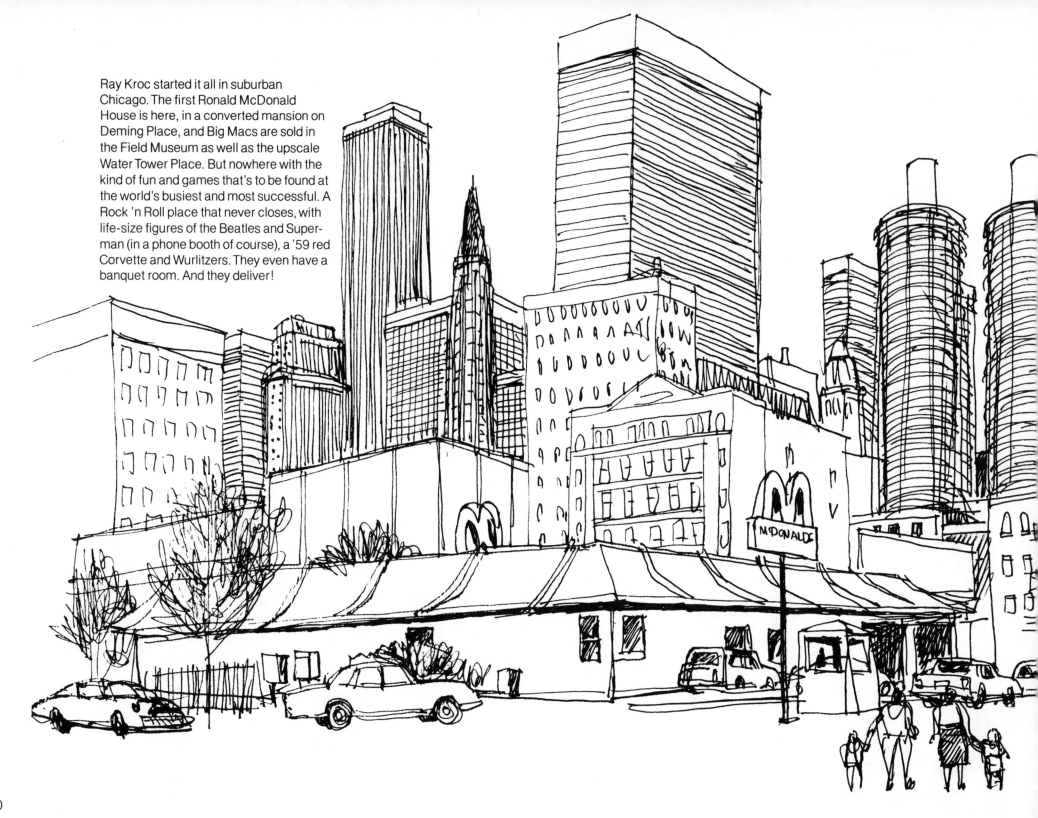

Ray Kroc started it all in suburban
Chicago. The first Ronald McDonald
House is here, in a converted mansion on
Deming Place, and Big Macs are sold in
the Field Museum as well as the upscale
Water Tower Place. But nowhere with the
kind of fun and games that's to be found at
the world's busiest and most successful. A
Rock 'n Roll place that never closes, with
life-size figures of the Beatles and Super-
man (in a phone booth of course), a '59 red
Corvette and Wurlitzers. They even have a
banquet room. And they deliver!

The Golden Ox, 1578 North Clybourn, is the heart of old Germantown, and is still serving superior German fare—bountiful, home-brewed soups (opt for the "leberknodel," the liver dumpling), wonderful wursts and wienerschnitzels with side dishes of creamed spinach and spaetzle a must.

GOLDEN OX

GOLDEN OX RESTAURANT.

DONALD'S AT ...RD AND CLARK.

101

During World War II, a footballer from Texas—he's in the College Hall of Fame—roared into town, started a pizzeria, and invented Chicago-style pizza—the deep-dish variety. The year was 1942 and the name Ike Sewall, but better known was the name on the sign—Pizzeria Uno at Wabash and Ohio. Then came Pizzeria Due and years later, franchising. So now pizza freaks all over the land know about Chicago's deep-dish delights.

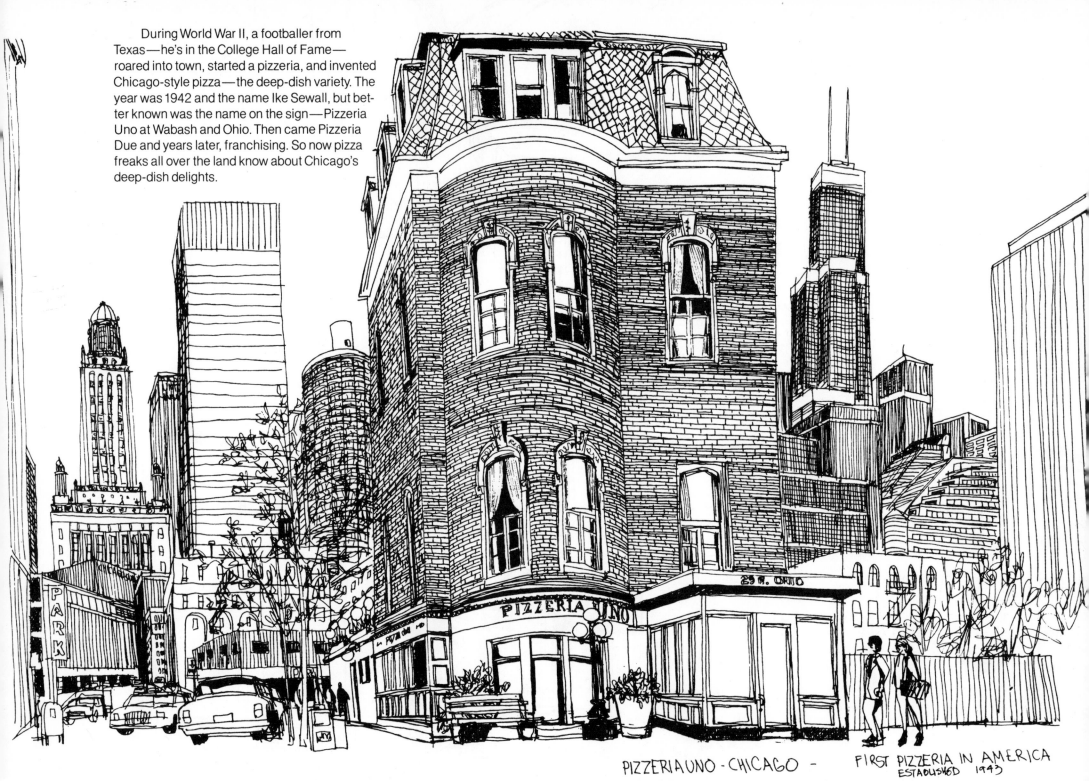

PIZZERIA UNO · CHICAGO ·

FIRST PIZZERIA IN AMERICA
ESTABLISHED 1943

BERGHOFFS
RESTAURANT

BINYON'S

Above: Our grandfathers discovered the place—probably because of the free lunch—and our fathers treated us to the stand-up pedestals and mouth-bending sandwiches. We came back on high school and college dates because the prices were right and today you can relive the experience, feasting on the sauerbraten and potato pancakes, the smoked pork loin and steins of the house beer, efficiently brought to the table by waiters of the old school. That's The Berghoff, 17 West Adams Street.

Right: Binyon's at 327 South Plymouth Court is another of the German survivors; but it's equally American in its preparation of solid food honestly prepared. Start with chopped liver and proceed to the garlic-heightened baked shrimp.

People at Play

And Chicagoans do play—hard and happily, indoors and out, on beaches and in boats. And they love their Bears and their Cubs, and they kept their White Sox. Chicago jazz has its own history and lore, and Chicago has been a theater town ever since its incorporation in 1837. What city in the world boasts a better symphony? Or such a generous expanse of lakefront greenery or shopping spreads as marvelous as the Magnificent Mile?

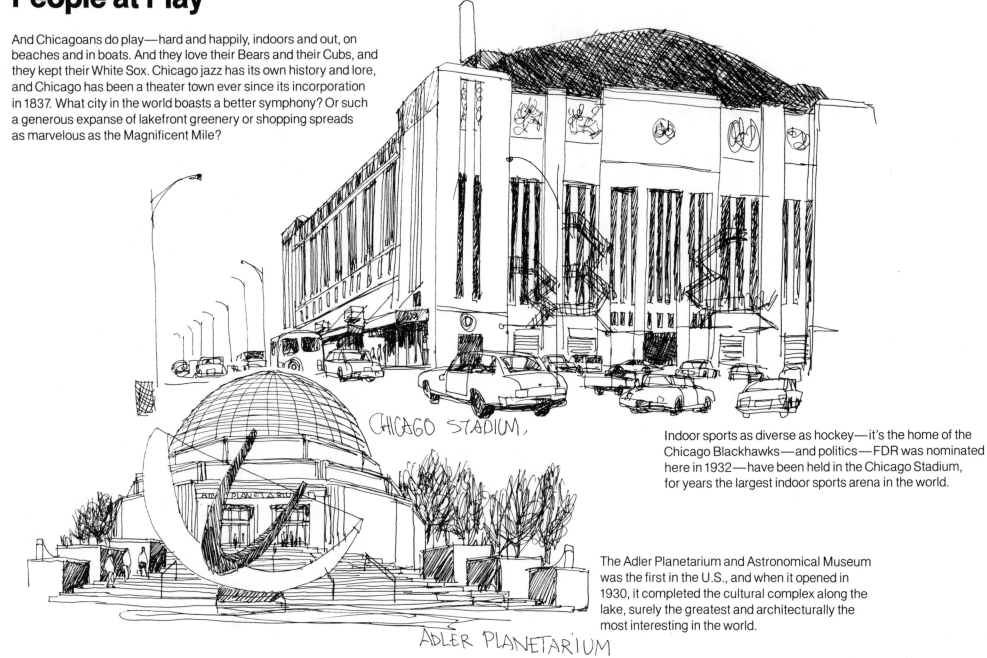

CHICAGO STADIUM.

ADLER PLANETARIUM

Indoor sports as diverse as hockey—it's the home of the Chicago Blackhawks—and politics—FDR was nominated here in 1932—have been held in the Chicago Stadium, for years the largest indoor sports arena in the world.

The Adler Planetarium and Astronomical Museum was the first in the U.S., and when it opened in 1930, it completed the cultural complex along the lake, surely the greatest and architecturally the most interesting in the world.

CIVIC OPERA HOUSE
HOME OF LYRIC OPERA

Michigan Avenue from the Art Institute, a stroller's delight.

106

North Michigan Avenue, with some of the most tempting
stores—and most powerful companies overhead—
to be found in the world.

McCormick Place, magnet for the many—to buy, to sell, to exhibit. It's the largest exhibition hall in the country.

CHICAGO AT McCORMICK PLACE.

330 N. JEFFERSON
AT WAYMAN STREET

Michigan Avenue—"probably destined to carry the heaviest movement of any street in the world." in the words of Burnham's 1909 Chicago Plan—sweeps across the broad expanse of the city with a great sense of style, and place.

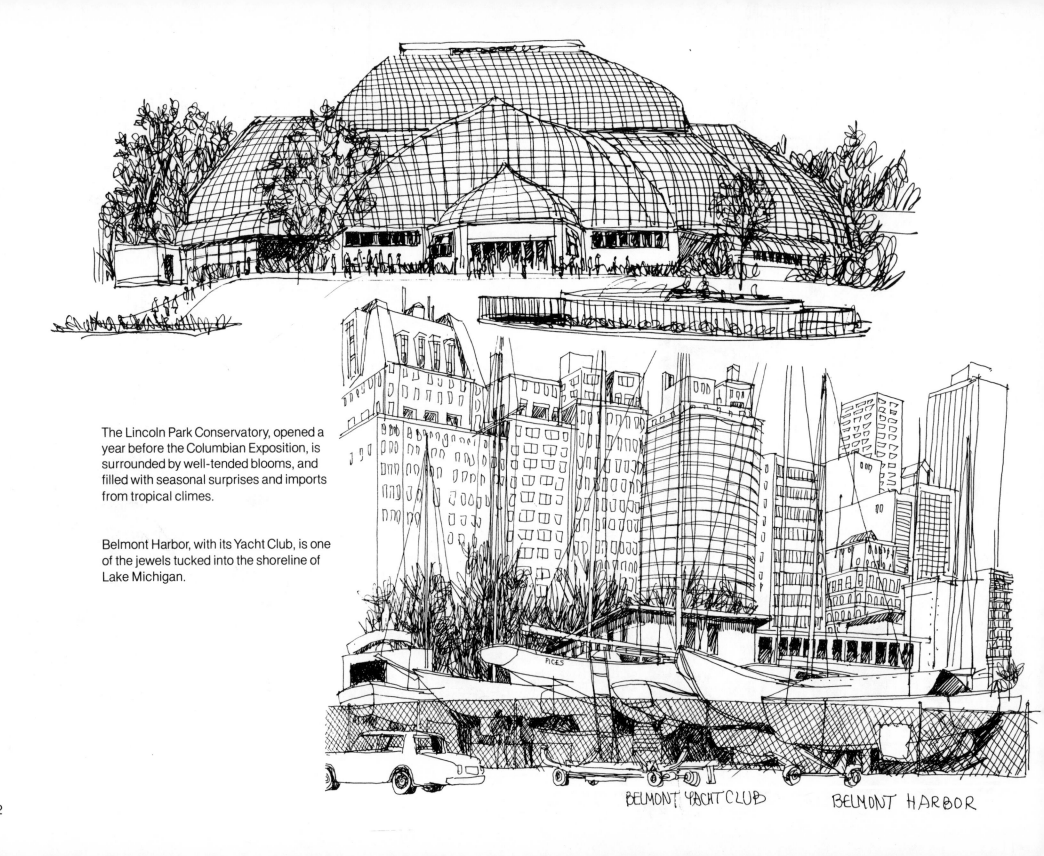

The Lincoln Park Conservatory, opened a year before the Columbian Exposition, is surrounded by well-tended blooms, and filled with seasonal surprises and imports from tropical climes.

Belmont Harbor, with its Yacht Club, is one of the jewels tucked into the shoreline of Lake Michigan.

BELMONT YACHT CLUB   BELMONT HARBOR

CHINATOWN

Chicago's Chinatown, complete with ceremonial entrance gate, masses of moo goo gai pan and red lanterns—
and telephone booths in pagodas.

The oldest zoo in the country and the first to have a year-round Children's Zoo, this Lincoln Park landmark, rambling through 35 acres and filled with over 2000 animals, birds and reptiles, started in 1868. Its Great Ape House has the finest assemblage of chimpanzees, gorillas and orangutans in the world.

Cafe Brauer in Lincoln Park is a great example of Prairie School Architecture. Opened in 1905, it's now in the middle of a major restoration, concentrating on bringing the building back to its original beauty. New restaurant concepts plus the restored Great Hall will make this one of the premiere places for special events. The paddle boats and snack bar will still be part of its charm.

OLN PARK ZOO

Lincoln Park's Farm in the Zoo is a new exhibit and it brings the country into the city, in a bright and hands-on educational manner.

FARM IN THE ZOO

The legendary heroes haunt this park—most beautiful in either league—and bring back the memories of better days starting with Grover Cleveland Alexander, Joe McCarthy, Kiki Cuyler, Rogers Hornsby, Hack Wilson, "Jolly Cholly" Grimm and Gabby Hartnett with his immortal "homer in the gloamin". And for diehard Cub fans—they are found all over the country—there's always next year. And a park full of lights.

WRIGLEY FIELD

117

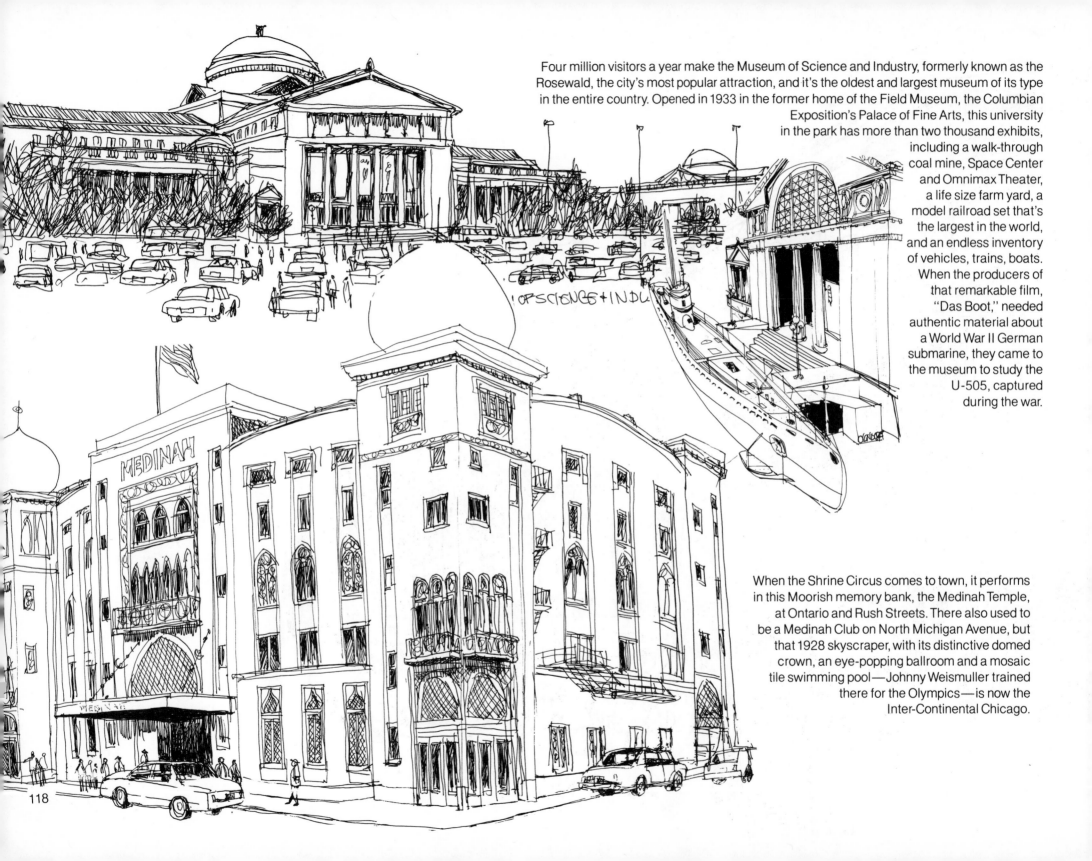

Four million visitors a year make the Museum of Science and Industry, formerly known as the Rosewald, the city's most popular attraction, and it's the oldest and largest museum of its type in the entire country. Opened in 1933 in the former home of the Field Museum, the Columbian Exposition's Palace of Fine Arts, this university in the park has more than two thousand exhibits, including a walk-through coal mine, Space Center and Omnimax Theater, a life size farm yard, a model railroad set that's the largest in the world, and an endless inventory of vehicles, trains, boats. When the producers of that remarkable film, "Das Boot," needed authentic material about a World War II German submarine, they came to the museum to study the U-505, captured during the war.

When the Shrine Circus comes to town, it performs in this Moorish memory bank, the Medinah Temple, at Ontario and Rush Streets. There also used to be a Medinah Club on North Michigan Avenue, but that 1928 skyscraper, with its distinctive domed crown, an eye-popping ballroom and a mosaic tile swimming pool—Johnny Weismuller trained there for the Olympics—is now the Inter-Continental Chicago.

Walgreen's on the corner and the born-again Chicago Theater alongside—two landmarks, both moving with the times. The Theater is a treasure trove, a restored tribute to the movie palace moguls, the masters of architectural fantasy, Abe and Barney Balaban and Sam Katz. Unequalled opulence and sheer escape with live stage shows and promotions galore are what Balaban and Katz delivered, and their Chicago theaters—first in the Midwest—could seat more people than all of Broadway combined.

CHICAGO THEATRE

Oldest park in the major leagues, built in 1910, is now finally being replaced. The Sox can look forward to brighter days in new surroundings.

Soldier Field—a six million dollar tribute in classic Greek style to the Chicago troops in World War I—
adds an athletic accent to the lakefront cultural campus and was envisioned in the 1909 Chicago Plan.
But of most importance is the fact that it's the home of the Chicago Bears.

COMISKEY PARK

Clubs

STANDARD CLUB

The club with what is generally acknowledged to be the best kitchen is The Standard, gathering place for Chicago's Jewish community.

Chicagoans who want to break their bread in more exclusive surroundings congregate in one or another of the clubs.

The Cliffdwellers' Club on the top of Orchestra Hall has been the artists' and intellectuals' hideout ever since it was organized after the completion of the building in 1905. Louis Sullivan and Frank Lloyd Wright were among the early members.

CLIFF DWELLERS AT ORCHESTRA HALL

The forerunners of Chicago's Union League Club were founded during the first years of the Civil War as a means to promote patriotism and loyalty to Lincoln and his cause. And there is still major attention given to the words of Rufus Choate's declaration—in painting and on the meal checks—that "We join ourselves to no party which does not carry the Flag and keep step to the Music of the Union." The sixth floor dining room of the club is called The Wigwam, named, not for the wealth of Indian paintings on the walls, but for a building a few blocks away, where Lincoln was nominated for President in 1860. There's a fine portrait of Lincoln in that room and elsewhere are other valuable Civil War renditions—part of the second largest art collection in the city.

UNION LEAGUE CLUB

For those movers and shakers on the Near North, there's the Racquet Club.

RACQUET CLUB

The University Club occupies
an imposing building on
Michigan Avenue, at the
corner of Monroe.

UNIVERSITY CLUB
AT MONROE & MICHIGAN

And in the shadow of the John Hancock Building there's the Casino Club, an old money retreat which adamantly refused to sell out to Big John no matter how high they pushed the price. They did, however, reluctantly agree to sell their tennis court.

ASINO CLUB

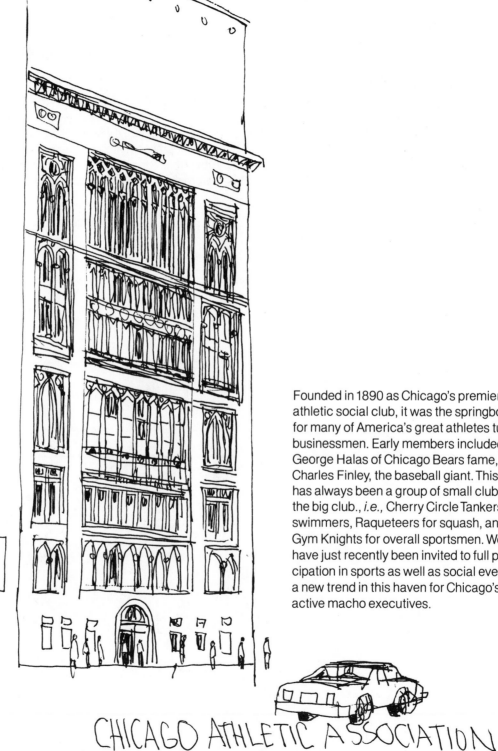

Founded in 1890 as Chicago's premiere athletic social club, it was the springboard for many of America's great athletes turned businessmen. Early members included George Halas of Chicago Bears fame, and Charles Finley, the baseball giant. This club has always been a group of small clubs within the big club., *i.e.,* Cherry Circle Tankers for swimmers, Raqueteers for squash, and the Gym Knights for overall sportsmen. Women have just recently been invited to full participation in sports as well as social events— a new trend in this haven for Chicago's sports active macho executives.

CHICAGO ATHLETIC ASSOCIATION

Modern Mecca

"When a history of Architecture in the United States shall have been written, it will be found that Chicago, synonymous in many minds with materialism, has been more potent in the development of architecture in this country than any other city." So wrote famed architecture critic Thomas Tallmadge. In 1921! Before the building boom of the 1920s. Before the post-World War II building boom. Before the 1970s and 1980s. Before the flowering of the Second Chicago School.

Trendy boutiques and a veritable gaggle of galleries opened in the old neighborhoods, and there were signs all along Oak, Clark and Lincoln Streets of tremendous revitalization in the 1970s and 80s.

OAK STREET.

New skyscrapers soared up from the flat land and soon the Drake Hotel, sparkling from its own facelift, found itself watched over by the three towers of One Magnificent Mile, finished in polished pink granite and strategically situated so there would be no sun block for those working on their tans at the Oak Street Beach.

The classics of the original Chicago School were reborn—such as the 1904 Railway Exchange Building on the corner of Michigan and Jackson. Daniel Burnham was the architect and he moved his offices to the seventeen-story building when it was completed.

The Inland Steel Building was the first stainless steel building in the country.

JACKSON AT MICHIGAN AVE

132

900 North Michigan Avenue, with its 58-story limestone and glass tower and eight-story base introduction, rivals Water Tower Place in sheer size, floor space and number of shops and snackeries. And this boasts the beautiful presence of Bloomingdale's. Another first for Chicago. It's the first Bloomie's in the Midwest.

BLOOMINGDALE'S MICHIGAN AVE.

STEEL BUILDING 1957

133

The pride and joy of Chicago's citizenry from the moment the terracotta tiles were bathed in light was—and is for present generations-the Wrigley Building along the Chicago River. It's a mounted clock tower reminiscent of Seville's historic Giralda and a monument of another era of tremendous expansion and architectural achievement.

Across the Avenue there rose at the same time the rigidly perpendicular Tribune Tower, a latter-day demonstration of those determined words by *Tribune* editor Joseph Medill the day after the Great Fire: "Chicago Shall Rise Again."

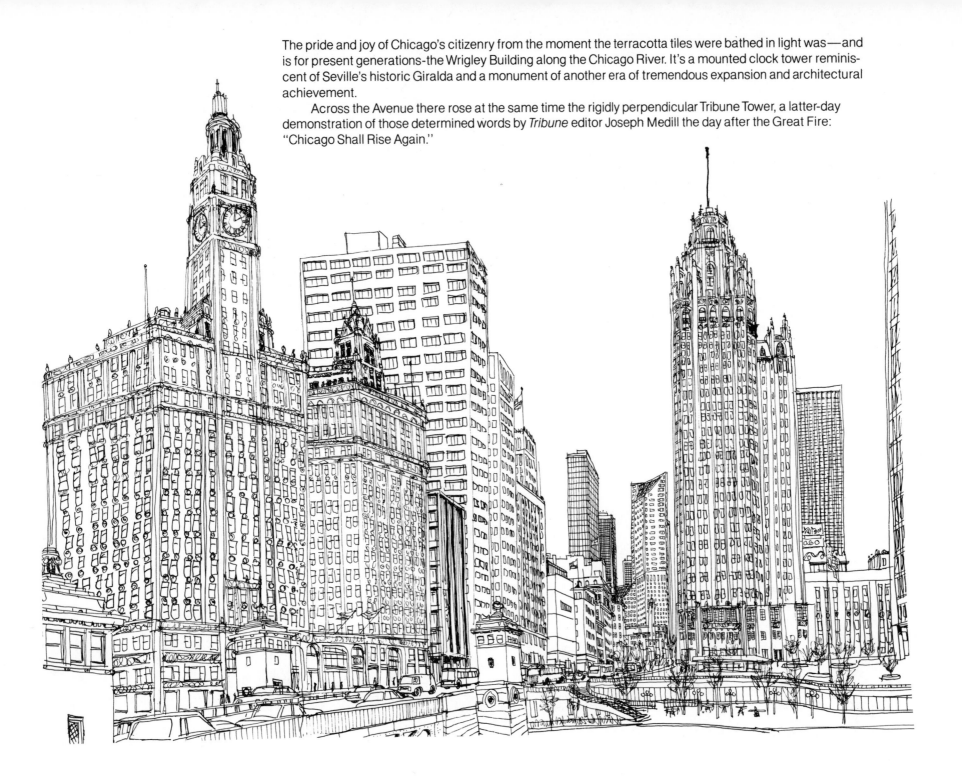

When Holabird and Root were working on the plans for the Board of Trade in the late 1920s, they were also completing those for the Palmolive Building at 919 North Michigan—for several years of identity crisis known as the Playboy Building.

Following gracefully a bend in the river—and ever so soothingly with its green glass—is the 333 West Wacker Drive Building, an eye and spirit-pleasing achievement of the firms Kohn Pedersen Fox and Perkins & Will.

333 WEST WACKER DRIVE

PALMOLIVE BUILDING 1928

135

The 1969 John Hancock Building, with its steel braces zigzagging across the hundred floors, is the second "Big John" in Chicago's history. The first was John Wentworth, who arrived in 1836 and checked in at 6'6" and 300 pounds—he had walked from Michigan City. That "Big John" was to become the youngest member of Congress and Chicago's first Republican mayor.

Hard hats and cranes were everywhere in evidence during the explosion of construction to match that after the Great Fire of 1871. Billions of dollars were being invested in office space and apartments, bringing thousands of Chicagoans and eager emigrés from elsewhere back to the heart of the city.

S. WACKER DRIVE

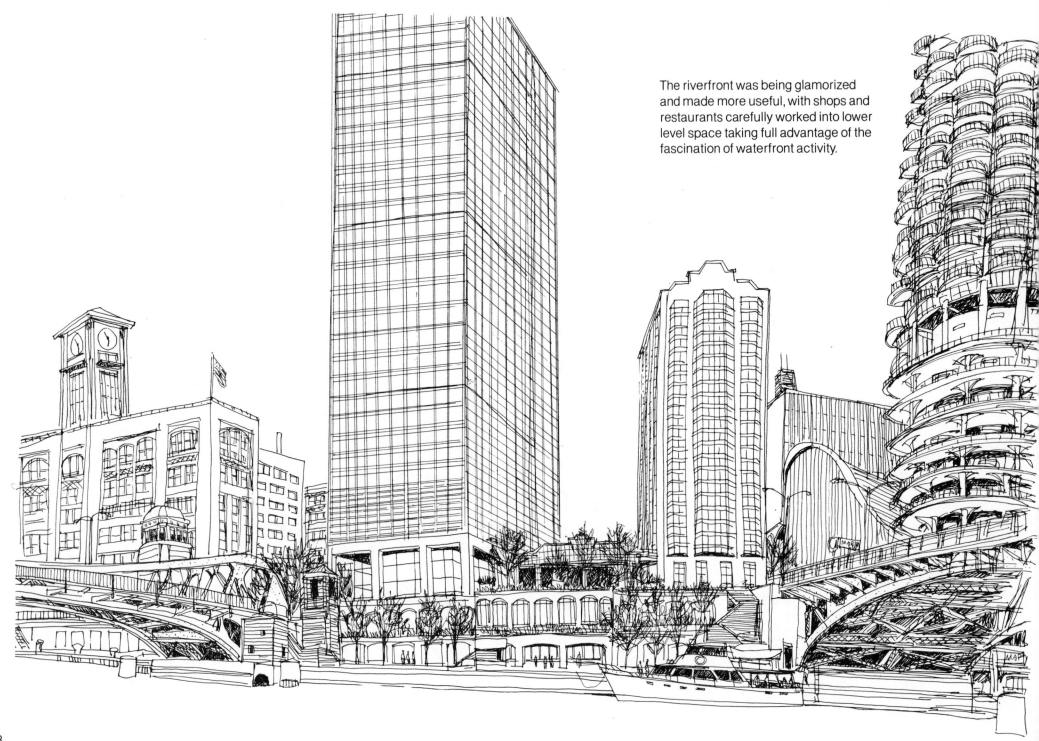

The riverfront was being glamorized and made more useful, with shops and restaurants carefully worked into lower level space taking full advantage of the fascination of waterfront activity.

On the northern bank of the river, between Clark and Dearborn Streets, there's Riverfront Park, a life-giving promenade between a local link in the Japanese Nikko Hotel chain, complete with several layers of shops and stores along the water, and Quaker Tower, a 35-story more or less Miesian clean-line linear statement that is sheathed in cooling glass of blue-green.

QUAKER TOWER
AT RIVERFRONT
PARK

OLENDORF

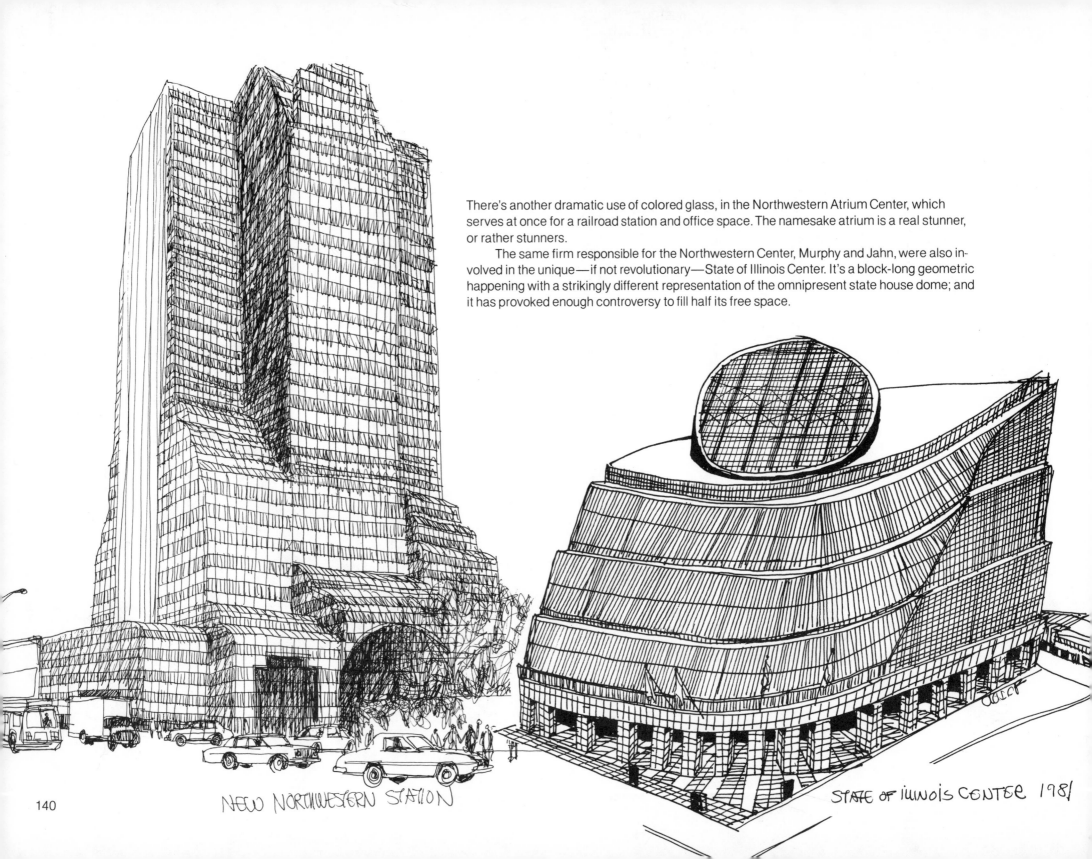

There's another dramatic use of colored glass, in the Northwestern Atrium Center, which serves at once for a railroad station and office space. The namesake atrium is a real stunner, or rather stunners.

The same firm responsible for the Northwestern Center, Murphy and Jahn, were also involved in the unique—if not revolutionary—State of Illinois Center. It's a block-long geometric happening with a strikingly different representation of the omnipresent state house dome; and it has provoked enough controversy to fill half its free space.

NEW NORTHWESTERN STATION

STATE OF ILLINOIS CENTER 1981

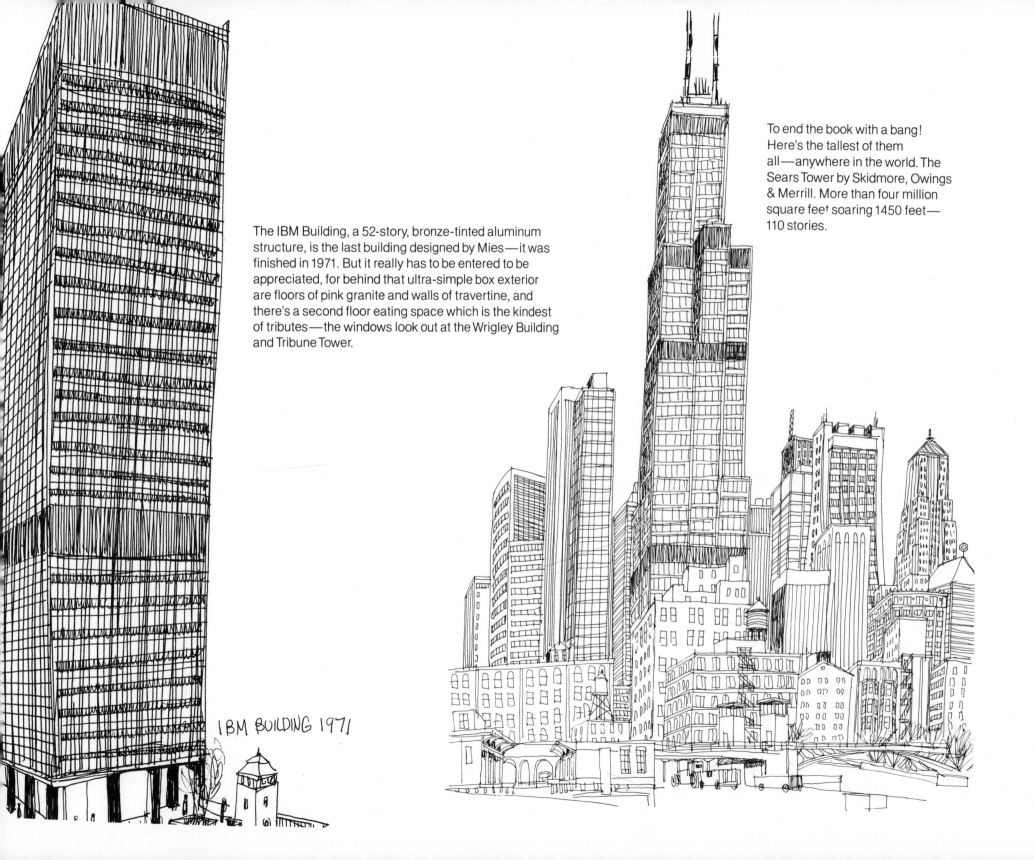

The IBM Building, a 52-story, bronze-tinted aluminum structure, is the last building designed by Mies—it was finished in 1971. But it really has to be entered to be appreciated, for behind that ultra-simple box exterior are floors of pink granite and walls of travertine, and there's a second floor eating space which is the kindest of tributes—the windows look out at the Wrigley Building and Tribune Tower.

To end the book with a bang! Here's the tallest of them all—anywhere in the world. The Sears Tower by Skidmore, Owings & Merrill. More than four million square feet soaring 1450 feet—110 stories.

IBM BUILDING 1971

CHICAGO RIVER

ΕΛΛΗΝΙΚΟΝ
ΜΑΓΑΖΙ

EARL OF OLDTOWN
CAFE & PUB

WELLS STREET